Judy Chicago is an artist, writer, teacher, and thinker whose work and philosophy have had an international impact on art and culture. Her most recent work is *Holocaust Project: From Darkness into Light*, a multimedia exhibition exploring the meaning of the Holocaust, which is scheduled to appear through 1997 in museums across America. The companion book, also titled *Holocaust Project*, is the author's fiercely personal record of her quest to imagine the unimaginable. She is best known for *The Dinner Party*, a collaborative, multimedia installation that presents a symbolic history of women in Western civilization through a series of thirty-nine place settings, set on a triangular banquet table forty-eight feet per side. *The Dinner Party* has traveled extensively throughout the United States and to five other countries, and it has been seen by approximately one million viewers during its fourteen exhibitions.

In the 1980s Chicago worked on the *Birth Project*, another collaborative effort. This series of needleworked images celebrating birth and creation in Western art was exhibited in a hundred venues around the United States. She then created *Powerplay*, a series of drawings, paintings, weaving, cast paper pieces, and bronzes that explore how male definitions of power affect the world in general and men in particular.

Other books by Chicago include *The Dinner Party*, *Embroidering Our Heritage*, and *Birth Project*. There have been four films made about the artist's work, and she has lectured widely to diverse audiences all over the world. She lives in New Mexico with her husband, photographer Donald Woodman.

THROUGH THE

THE

My Struggle as

BY

WITH AN INTRODUCTION BY

FLOWER

A Woman Artist

JUDY CHICAGO

ANAIS NIN

PENGUIN BOOKS

PENGUIN BOOKS
Published by the Penguin Group
Penguin Books USA Inc., 375 Hudson Street,
New York, New York 10014, U.S.A.
Penguin Books Ltd, 27 Wrights Lane, London W8 5TZ, England
Penguin Books Australia Ltd, Ringwood, Victoria, Australia
Penguin Books Canada Ltd, 10 Alcorn Avenue,
Toronto, Ontario, Canada M4V 3B2
Penguin Books (N.Z.) Ltd, 182–190 Wairau Road,
Auckland 10, New Zealand

Penguin Books Ltd, Registered Offices:
Harmondsworth, Middlesex, England

First published in the United States of America
by Doubleday & Company, Inc. 1975
Published in Penguin Books 1993

1 3 5 7 9 10 8 6 4 2

LIBRARY OF CONGRESS CATALOGING IN PUBLICATION DATA
Chicago, Judy, 1939–
Through the flower: my struggle as a woman artist/ by Judy
Chicago; with an introduction by Anaïs Nin.
p.   cm.
Originally published: Garden City, N.Y.: Doubleday Books, 1975.
Includes bibliographical references and index.
ISBN 0 14 02.3122 6
1. Chicago, Judy, 1939–   . 2. Artists—United States—Biography.
I. Title.
N6537.C48A2   1993
700'.92—dc20   93–19313

Printed in the United States of America
Set in Baskerville

Preface to the New Edition

‿

It is 1993; nearly fifty years since I began studying art; over thirty-five years since I left the city of my birth to go to college in California; almost thirty years since I had my first solo show; even longer than that since my first husband died; fourteen years since my second husband, Lloyd, and I divorced; and over seven years since I remarried. (They say three's a charm, and my marriage to photographer Donald Woodman seems to be proving this proverb true.)

Through the Flower was first published in 1975. It went on to enjoy several printings in paperback and was also published in Japan, England, and Germany. Its worldwide distribution helped build an international audience for my work, and when it went out of print in the eighties I was greatly distressed. I am grateful to Mindy Werner and Penguin Books for reissuing *Through the Flower,* particularly since I frequently receive letters from teachers and students searching for it.

It never occurred to me I'd be a writer as well as an artist, even though I am about to publish my fifth book, *The Holo-*

caust Project: From Darkness into Light, which will accompany a traveling exhibition Donald and I recently completed. This body of work—eight years in the making— extends my concern for women's oppression into an examination of the victim experience as seen through the prism of the Jewish experience of the Holocaust. Next year I plan to write my sixth book, a sequel to this book, which will chronicle my evolution since 1972, when I began *Through the Flower.*

When I wrote this autobiography, I intended it as a primer for young women artists, something to aid them in their development. By documenting my own struggle, I had hoped to spare them the anguish of "reinventing the wheel," which my studies in women's history had taught me was done again and again by women, specifically because we have not had access to our foremothers' experience and achievements.

Many years ago I was included in a traveling exhibition titled "Creativity," sponsored by Chevron and now permanently installed in the Seattle Science Center. One of the designers, the late Stephen Hamilton, told me that an essential criteria for inclusion in the show was that the creative person had to have documented their own creative process, which he said that few women had done.

Since writing *Through the Flower,* I've learned that it is not true that women haven't tried to "pass on" their experiences. But as I said in Johanna Demetraka's film "Right Out of History: The Making of Judy Chicago's *The Dinner Party,*" our efforts haven't been adequately represented in the history books or museums, nor preserved as part of human cultural memory. Generally, instead of being "written into" history, we have been "written out."

The story of *The Dinner Party*—i.e., its creation, its reception, and the influence of this symbolic history of women in Western civilization—will be examined in an upcoming (1995) exhibition at UCLA. Suffice it to say that when I undertook the six-year effort to create *The Dinner Party,* I did so in the hope that by demonstrating the way in which women's achievements had been repeatedly erased from the historic record, I would be able to break this cycle. My goal in 1974— when I started the first drawings for the plates—remains the same today: to ensure that this tribute to women becomes a permanent part of our cultural heritage, so that the courage and wisdom of the women represented can provide a foundation for future generations to build a respect for women's achievements that is sorely lacking today.

After completing *The Dinner Party,* I began to do research on birth images. I wanted to use the birth process as a metaphor for the creation of life. Much to my surprise, I found there were few paintings or sculptures in the history of Western art—and until quite recently no pictures at all—of the actual moment of birth. Despite the fact that birth is so obviously a universal experience and central to most women's lives, it has rarely been depicted or described. This forces every woman to experience privately and often abjectly what could be a triumphant confrontation with the life process itself.

The *Birth Project* grew out of my recognition of what this lack of images means: i.e., that which is not imaged exists outside of what is considered part of the "universal" human experience. The *Birth Project* continued the participatory nature of *The Dinner Party,* but instead of everyone working in my studio, most of the participants worked at home, though still under my supervision. As in *The Dinner Party,* the images were mine but the process of translating or executing them into a range of needle techniques drew upon the talents and abilities of the individual needleworkers. The extended process of executing these pieces often engaged the needleworker's family, friends, and neighbors in dialogue, if not in the actual stitching. These works were not conceived to be shown all together but, rather, to be viewed as unique pieces, individually or in small groupings. They were exhibited all over America between 1985 and 1987 in some hundred venues. Since then, individual works have been placed in museums and institutions around the country. This is consistent with my goal of introducing art into the life of the community in a way that allows people to see images they can relate to.

As I work with people year after year, I realize how little most people know about art. I have always believed that art is important—in fact central—to human life. The spirit of art is always affirming, even when it deals with painful realities, for the act of making an image transforms that pain into something meaningful. This act is what has always sustained me, no matter how difficult my life has sometimes been. That the products of my artmaking activity have reached and affected so many other people has given me the strength to go on.

I will forever be indebted to Anaïs Nin for encouraging me to write. She read a short essay I wrote in 1971 titled "My Struggles as a Woman Artist," and when I met her soon after its publication I was startled by her enthusiasm for the piece.

Recently, a number of young women have begun studying and interning with me and, sadly, I have learned how many of them continue to be thwarted in their development, especially by being deprived of an understanding of and pride in their heritage as women. I dedicate this book to them in the hope that they will derive some of the same inspiration from it that I was privileged to receive from Anaïs.

Contents

Introduction

This is a remarkable book, which is invaluable for all women, artist and nonartist. It is a blend of very human, very honest, utterly revealing personal history, with the larger issues of creativity, with woman's problems throughout the history of art. It includes a panoramic view of the history of women artist, but the struggle, the humanity, and the honesty are applicable to all women. I have been saying for many years that we need articulate women. It was Judy Chicago's extraordinary articulateness that impressed me and made me encourage her to write. Not all of us would have the privilege of talking with her, of learning about her life, her work, her teaching. She is all the more to be trusted because behind her words lie the achievement of a recognized painter, one who has expressed both power and subtlety, originality and daring. It is immensely moving to see her concern for the development of other women. Every insight she learned she needed to share. She gave a lesson in humanity when she relinquished the concept of the infallibility of the leader and sought to teach by exchange and by dialogue. Her generosity was particularly admirable because she had the qualities of leadership: She moves into the future, she conceptualizes the future, she is capable of synthesis. I find it rather touching that working with some young women artists, she taught them so well that after a while, with human lack of generosity, they began to resent her power to inspire, to awaken them from their lethargy and lack of initiative. The whole conflict of inspiration lies there. The pioneer has courage and moves forward. The passive ones follow. Then they resent the "leader" who gives them a life they could not find for themselves.

Another generous quality in Judy, which is the sign of the creative personality, is her continuous self-induced movement forward. Disappointments, betrayals, obstacles, nothing deters her from her dynamic flowering, "through the flower." When she gives the history of her childhood, the history of her marriage, the history of her work and of her teaching, it is all amazingly fecund; it is a lesson in courage and a lesson in the need of creativity to be applied to one's life as well as one's work. They are inseparable. I consider this the particular contribution of woman, the ability to blend the personal with the objective beyond the personal. Judy does this perfectly. The childhood and adolescence are diffused, confused, honest. The marriage is not a miracle born of romanticism, but a creation born of goodwill and love on both sides. The work requires fortitude. And when heart, intuition, emotion have played their part, the intellect can make a synthesis.

The book encompasses the history of women creators. It englobes universal social factors. It situates the struggle of one woman both as a symbol and as a representative of many. It indicates the pursuit of a center, a strength that is gained. There is so much self-creation in this life that it proves Jung's assertion that our second birth is our own achievement. This is a unique achievement. She is a leader in the best sense. She shows the way; she shows the tools and the personal integrity and persistence required. She admits her moments of confusion, and weakness, but she also demonstrates the moments of endurance, spiritedness. In fact, it is her spirit that infuses the book with an energy that is contagious. I hope all women will read it. Both the life-giving energy and the broad vision will give birth to woman's pride in herself.

ANAÏS NIN

THROUGH
THE FLOWER

I do not delude myself, as Man does, that I create in proud isolation. . . . Woman's creation, far from being like Man's, must be exactly like her creation of children; that is, it must come out of her own blood, englobed by her womb, nourished with her own milk. It must be a human creation, of flesh, it must be different from Man's abstractions.

Anaïs Nin, from the *Diaries*

1

My Childhood

I was born at the Michael Reese Hospital in Chicago, Illinois, in 1939, at the end of the Depression. My mother tells a story about wearing a big bow on her bulging stomach during her pregnancy, signifying her delight at carrying me. My first memory is when I was a year and a half old. I see myself in my crib, red-faced and crying, and my mother, dressed in a navy blue suit and matching beret, going out the door to work. Throughout my childhood, my mother worked, a situation which, I suppose, gave me a sense that women "did" something in the world. I was left with a series of housekeepers. The one I remember the best was named Oradie Blue, who was black and who inspired a game that my father frequently played with me. He would put me on his knee and tell me a story that always began: "Oradie Blue was walking down the street and met John Green. Then they continued walking together and met Norman White, to whom they talked for a while. Then Oradie Blue and Norman White left John Green and went to a restaurant where they met Mary Black." This story/game, combined with a constant stream of visitors of all races in our house, helped me to understand that color was not a significant factor in dealing with people.

I loved my father and liked to play the games that he continually devised for me, games that trained me in logic, mathematics, and gave me a sense of human values. I have many memories of him and of my mother, but many of my recollections are mixed with and indistinguishable from stories told to me about my childhood, for I quickly became a focus of attention in my parents' active life. They were both involved in politics, and our house was the center for political activity in the neighborhood. I was too young to understand the meaning of this activity, but I loved the constant discussions, usually led by my father, who sat in a rust-colored velvet chair, next to a window, talking intensely, his fingers stained with the nicotine of his ever-present cigarette, his legs crossed, their whiteness showing beneath his slightly raised trouser leg. I was allowed to participate in many of the activities, and "Judy" stories are still told by my mother's friends about my often amusing antics.

I possess fragmented glimpses of myself, my parents, my nurses, and the house on Bittersweet Place that we moved into when I was two, where I lived until I was eighteen. I didn't talk until I was two and a half, which was a source of great concern to my parents, to whom talking represented their main link to life. My mother frequently remarked about how my father and she always talked to each other in restaurants, while other married couples seemed to sit in stony silence. I learned the value that my parents placed on verbalizing, and, after my reluctant beginning, began to talk in such a way that grown-ups always remarked at my precocity, which pleased my parents enormously.

My parents were very casual about nudity, and I often took baths with my father, at least when I was two or three.

Several years ago, my mother reminded me of a story about one of these baths that made me quite uneasy. Apparently, I wanted to be like my father from the time I was young. One day, in the bath, I pointed to his penis and said, "When I grow up, I'm going to have one of those." My father laughed and said "Yes, if you're a good girl, you'll have *one* of those. If you're a bad girl you'll have a lot of them." He repeated this story several times to various friends in front of me. The story always made me feel guilty about wanting to be like my father, and yet, I admired him and loved him and he was always the center of attention at parties, and everybody said he was really smart. Thinking about this story, I realized that it was not that I wanted to be a boy, but rather, that I wanted to be a person like my father. It was a long time before I was to realize that one's sex was supposed to determine one's personality, interests, and options.

Because my mother worked, and because I saw women participating fully in all the discussions that went on in the house, I grew up with the sense that I could do what I wanted and be what I wanted. As a girl child, I was encouraged to be honest and direct, affectionate and trusting. I had two female cousins, both ten years older than I, both in college, who came to the house frequently, were very active intellectually, and provided positive role models for me.

When I was three, I began drawing, and my mother, who had wanted to be a dancer, gave me a lot of encouragement. She told me many stories about her life prior to her marriage, when she went to the Jewish People's Institute and mingled with musicians, poets, and other creative people. Throughout my childhood, she told me colorful tales about the creative life, particularly when I was sick in bed, and these stories contributed to my developing interest in art, for, from the time I was young, I wanted to be an artist. My father, on the other hand, could never relate to my artistic impulse, so it was to my mother that I brought my artistic achievements and to my father that I brought my intellectual ones.

My brother Ben was born when I was five and a half years old. I remember the day my mother brought him home from the hospital. There he lay, red-faced and screaming, on my parents' big bed, which, every Sunday afternoon, I claimed for my own when my father and I listened to radio programs. Ben was born with a vestigial stomach, which caused him great difficulty in ingesting food. He cried a lot, and it seemed that his arrival introduced strife into our household. I did not realize that there were other factors operating in my parents' lives that were creating tensions and strains. My parents' politics were extremely left-wing, although how radical I only knew when I was twelve or thirteen years old. They had been involved in politics throughout the thirties and forties. My father was a union organizer, and after the war, shortly after my brother was born, became the victim of the anti-Communist sentiments that ultimately manifested in Joseph McCarthy and his witch-hunts. When I was six, an FBI agent forced his way into the house when I was home alone with my brother. My mother arrived before he could question me, and she angrily chased him away. He had been trying to find out about my parents' political sentiments, which I really didn't understand then anyway. I hadn't realized that he was an FBI agent or that we were being harassed, as I was completely protected from everything but the emotional ramifications of the events in my parents' lives. Things were happening that I didn't understand, and they were disturbing, but, at the same time, much of my life was still untouched by my parents' problems.

In 1947, I began to go to the Art Institute of Chicago for art lessons. Every Saturday, I took the No. 53 Bus and arrived at a world in which I could put aside the precocious daughter that my father loved and the confused girl that I was becoming and lose myself in the enchantment of drawing and painting. I used to walk up the steps between the great lions that guard the doorway of the museum and enter the large auditorium where classes were held. When I was nine, I switched to the Junior School, where classes were smaller, and which I attended until I was eighteen years old. I used to go upstairs to the galleries, where I would wander through the paintings, stopping often in front of the Monet haystacks and the beautiful Seurat. When I was about eleven, I became fascinated with Toulouse-Lautrec and the way he used reds, dotting them around the painting so that your eye was forced to travel around and around until it had absorbed the entire picture. At the time, I gave no thought to the fact that, while I was studying the color, the images of women painted by artists like Lautrec were also penetrating my psyche, later to confuse me, the artist, who wanted to paint, with me, the woman, who, I learned through these paintings, was supposed to be the model.

My father had a large, quarrelsome, generous family, one or another of whom we visited regularly. My father, mother, brother, and I used to take the streetcar on Saturday. During the trip, we played games invented by my father, identifying objects on the street, counting different kinds of animals, any sort of game which, in my father's estimation, would help us build our powers of observation. Usually we went to see one or another of my father's sisters, where we ate boiled chicken or, my favorite, vanilla pudding with strawberries, served by my Aunt Rose, whose hand shook so nervously that, when she served matzo ball soup, I always expected a catastrophe.

By 1948, my father had been driven out of the union by the threat of an investigation that would probably have resulted in a jail sentence. Rather than face that, he decided to try to keep the family together by quitting his job, leaving the union, and going to work as an insurance salesman. But, losing the work that provided his life with meaning was hard on him, so hard that he began to get sick. For the next five years, he slowly deteriorated, often coming home from work early. I'd return from school and find my father sitting in the rust-colored velvet chair, dressed in a robe, smoking his Chesterfields, reading or listening to the radio. I didn't know why he was home, but I knew that other fathers didn't do that. I began to think that there was something wrong with him, especially when I overheard my aunts talking to him or my mother, implying that my father's statements about not feeling well, about having a "bellyache," were not true. All this made me doubt my father, but at the same time, I loved him deeply, and at school, I began to say: "My father thinks this and my father thinks that," as if to reinforce his declining authority.

When I was eleven, I had a boyfriend named Sandy, who was very smart in school. He took me to the Chicago Theater to see a movie and a stage show. While we were watching the movie, he put his arm around me, and I felt like a burning ember was on my shoulders. I was afraid that people in the audience would notice and think that I was a terrible girl, because, despite my parents' liberal attitudes, I had remained very naïve about sex. My mother insists that she explained the facts of life to me when I was six, but I think that her explanation was so technical that I didn't connect it with my real life. I remember my friend Paula providing an explanation about sex when I was nine and she was eleven. I was sitting with her and her friend on the porch of Paula's north Side home. They were talking about rape. I asked them what that meant, and Paula replied: "That's when a man makes you fuck him." Not knowing what the word "fuck" meant, the explanation went over my head. Later in Paula's room, I pursued the discussion. Paula explained to me that "fuck" meant "when a man puts his thing in your thing." Then, thoughtfully, she added: "People do it when they love each other." I was satisfied with that information until I was fourteen, when one of my cousins, who was younger than I, amplified these curious facts with her explanation of an erection.

I had had an unpleasant sexual experience when I was six, but I had not told my parents about it. I had a friend in the building in which we lived, a boy named Charles, who was four years older than I. He was pale and thin and wore wire rim spectacles. He locked me in a car one day and tried to molest me. I remember him pulling my blouse open and making me feel very frightened. I screamed and threatened to tell his mother, of whom he was terrified, and he finally let me out of the car. This memory is confused with another event that occurred when I was nine. I went to visit some relatives in a small town in southern Illinois. I was taken to see my Uncle Harry, my father's oldest brother, who was sick. He was lying on the bed, naked except for a pair of undershorts, completely paralyzed, with no cover to hide his withered body, almost blue in color. This pale, thin specter frightened me and somehow became connected in my mind with Charles' translucent white skin and the frightening experience in the car, probably because my uncle also wore wire rim glasses. My aunt forced me to kiss my uncle, and the next day he died. My father came and sent me home while he made the funeral arrangements. I was left with some strange fantasies about sex and death and my own needs which, combined with some of the images of devouring women in the paintings at the Art Institute, made me feel, later in my life, that my needs were threatening and my power devastating.

I began to develop breasts at twelve, and I remember one day when I was trying on a new bathing suit, and my mother made me parade in front of my father, who suddenly looked at me in a new way. It was as if he saw me as a sexual creature for the first time. It perplexed me, pleased me, and embarrassed me all at once. I had, as I mentioned, a very unclear picture of my own sexuality, and spent endless hours with my girlfriends discussing whether our parents "really did it." About the same time, I had my first real argument with my father concerning the high school I was to attend. In the early fifties in Chicago, high school students frequently obtained "passes" to go to schools out of their district. All of my friends were applying for passes to go to Senn High School, an all-Jewish school. My father, without explanation, forbade me to apply for a pass. I began arguing furiously with him, as the tears poured down my face. He was unusually intractable, and I don't know why he didn't just explain the reason for his refusal. It seemed that the pass system was the way Chicago dealt with the black problem. White students, who, because of the location of their houses, would ordinarily go to schools with blacks, were given passes to go to all-white schools. In our neighborhood, this system was used to keep schools Jewish and Gentile. As it turned out, the pass system was stopped that year because of legal pressure, and I and all my Jewish friends went to what had formerly been a Gentile school. My father's reluctance to explain the political basis for the pass system was probably linked up to the larger issue of his dilemma as a radical in the America of the fifties.

He had never spoken directly to me about his political beliefs. Growing up, I witnessed many discussions in my house about the injustices in the world, and I knew that my father was trying, in the unions, to improve working conditions and increase wages. But McCarthyism made all left-wing activity suspect, and I guess my father felt the need to make me understand what was happening to him. One night, shortly before my thirteenth birthday, my father came into my room. He sat down and asked me if I had heard the word "Communist." I showed him a copy of our weekly school newspaper, called *The Weekly Reader*. On the front page, there was a cartoon showing horrible, bloated yellow men thrusting bayonets into young, blond American boys. Those awful-looking yellow men were "Communists," according to this text.

My father explained to me that often, people who were trying to change the world, to improve it, were called "Communists" as a way of making it seem that they were doing something wrong. I said, somewhat cautiously, that it must be the people who *didn't* want to change things who were bad, not the people who were trying to make things better. My father seemed pleased by my statement, and for some reason, perhaps the intensity of my father's manner, I began to cry. He spoke to me that night about his desire to change the condition of black people in America, to abolish poverty, to expand educational opportunities for poor people, and to try to make the place he worked more humane. He tried to make me see that being called a name was not the most terrible thing in the world, but I didn't want my wonderful father to be associated with those ugly, bloated men in the school paper. Even though I understood that his goals were good, I was afraid that other people might not understand. When I went to school the next day, I felt that I could never tell anyone what my father had told me the previous evening. Everything in my upbringing had encouraged me to look up to and love my father, and yet, at school, anyone who was trying to change things was called a "Communist" and considered a "bad guy." I felt suddenly and completely alienated from my schoolmates, but I learned from that experience that the world's evaluation of a person might not be at all consistent with who that person really was, a lesson that was to serve me well in my own life.

Either during the night of the talk with my father or somewhere close in time to that evening, my father told me he was going into the hospital for an operation. I imagine that his sickness had impelled him to discuss his politics with me. The doctors had finally discovered the source of his continuing pain. They had found an ulcer, which required the removal of part of his stomach. I remember sitting on the steps of my house with my brother when my father went off. We stayed with one of our aunts, where many of the relatives came and went for the next five days. We didn't see my mother at all, as she was at the hospital. It was not until we'd been at my aunt's for three days that I had any idea of the seriousness of my father's condition. My Aunt Enid, my father's closest sister, told me that my father was very sick. I can remember myself asking in a shaky, frightened voice: "He couldn't die, could he?," feeling sure that she would say, "No, of course not." Instead, she answered, "Yes." Two days later, Ben and I were told that our father had died. From that moment until perhaps a year later, I have no clear memories of my reactions. I know that a long time after his death, I was riding on the elevated train and I saw his picture in my wallet and I cried and cried and I knew, with a terrible certainty, that I'd never see him again.

My mother didn't want us to go to the funeral. I guess she felt that we would witness some pretty terrible things, as my father's family was wont to blame life's tragedies on one or another of the family members. Perhaps it was a good decision, I don't know. All that I do know is that my father just walked out of our life with no warning and never came back. The only thing my mother ever said, as she couldn't be there to tell us of his death, was that he screamed at the end, out of his oxygen tent: "I don't want to die, I don't want to die," words which I cannot write, even now, without crying.

It was only later that I was to learn the details of his death: how the doctor opened his abdomen and discovered that all of his organs were matted together with adhesions and so inflamed that there was not enough healthy tissue to sustain the excising of part of his stomach. The adhesions had been caused many years before, when he was young and had suffered a ruptured appendix before the discovery of penicillin. Forced to stay in bed for many months, his insides slowly grew together, and thirty years later, when he developed an ulcer, became so infected that he suffered severe pain that could not be diagnosed. So, as my mother says, the operation was successful and the patient died.

My adolescence was spent in a repressed, painful confusion, struggling to try to make sense out of what had happened, trying to reconcile the wonderful, generous father I loved with the terrible word "Communist," which, in 1953, had all the connotations of the devil. I blamed myself for his death, going over every word of our argument about the pass system, trying to see if I perhaps had said something terrible to him, something that could have caused him to die. I examined our conversation on that last night: Had I disappointed him, is that why he died? I remembered that when I was three, I had gotten angry at my father and screamed at him: "I hate you, I hate you, I wish you would die." I had kissed my uncle, and the next day he died. Perhaps I could make people die by wishing it or by doing something wrong. Blaming myself alternated with trying somehow to keep my father alive, to push away the pain of his death. I used to visit my cousin Peggy, who worshiped my father. It was with her that I carried on the true occupation of my teens. For endless hours, we talked about my father. She told me stories about him, repeated statements he had made. From the age of thirteen to eighteen, I visited her repeatedly, always for the same reason: to be with the father I had lost, until finally, when I graduated from high school, I had to go two thousand miles away to get away from the past that I could not resolve.

During these years, my mother, who was not well herself, struggled with the task of being both father and mother to her children. Her income was supplemented by my father's insurance, and we managed to eke by. I will always be grateful that my mother never asked me to sacrifice my own development to make life easier for her. She helped me through college and encouraged me to make the best life I could for myself, despite the fact that some of her friends tried to make me feel that I should quit school and go to work to ease my mother's burden. But she was determined to provide for herself and her children, and she did.

My teens were a blur. My most vivid memories are of my visits with my cousin Peggy, and my mind jumps from the death of my father to the day when I was twenty-one and I sat in a chair in a therapist's office and began to talk about my father's death, trying to come out of the past and make contact with the present by releasing the grief that I had so long ago turned inward upon myself and that finally put me in the hospital with a bleeding ulcer the size of a fifty-cent piece that had perforated into my pancreas.

Although I had a hard time in high school because of all the repressed grief, outwardly I seemed to function well—so well, in fact, that most people I knew assumed that I was handling my father's death quite easily. Little did they know. I got good grades, continued my art lessons, and had lots of friends, though I was not part of the "popular" crowd and was not asked to join the "Laurels," which was the Jewish club, probably because I couldn't afford the number of cashmere sweaters that was required. Instead, I spent the time with some other Jewish boys and girls who were also not accepted into the Jewish clique. We read books and listened to music. I became involved with the Student Council and encountered some attitudes among the male students that I didn't understand until I was an adult. Many of them seemed to find my directness and assertiveness threatening, and they made comments about my being "bossy," which made me feel bad. But I tried not to pay much attention to their statements, and it never occurred to me that the boys' resistance to my leadership might have anything to do with my sex.

When I was fifteen or sixteen, I became involved with a group from another school and soon met Tommy, who became my first real boyfriend, not counting my seventh-grade romance with Sandy. Tommy went to an upper-middle-class high school and was older than I, giving me a little status at my school and also an excuse for my lack of popularity. Later, I found out that my classmates thought I was into my own thing, as they knew about my continuing classes at the Art Institute, and believed that I was sort of above all of the things with which they were concerned. This, of course, was not true, although I was glad that my dignity had somehow remained intact. Actually, I wanted nothing more than to be accepted into the popular group, and it caused me great pain to be unpopular.

Anyway, Tommy was a sweet boy who, interestingly enough, had an undiagnosable stomach condition, which frequently kept him home from school, where he sat around in a robe reading and watching TV. He adored me and was really nice to me. I had my first orgasm with him, but, of course, I didn't know what it was. It was on New Year's Eve. I was sixteen, and we were dry-humping on the couch.

Suddenly I experienced a great flash, which frightened me. I burst into tears and fell on the floor moaning, "I must be a whore, I must be a whore." I guess my confusion about sex was so great that I assumed that anything that intense must be bad. Nonetheless, I pursued the sensation, discovering that if Tommy stroked my buttocks and I squeezed my thighs together, it felt quite good and I would then feel relaxed enough to quit petting, which was *all* that "good girls" did in the fifties. The sexual mores of my generation were very peculiar. Everyone petted and everyone denied it, asserting that they only necked. If anyone admitted to petting, it was only to say that they petted above the waist. No one, but no one, went all the way.

I went with Tommy for a year or two. Then, one day, my mother's friend brought a university student named Allen to our house. He was about twenty-three to my seventeen and, as I wanted to impress him, I trotted out the behavior I had developed for my father. I performed intellectually, dazzling him with my use of long words, and in general coming on in a way that must have been ridiculous. However, he *was* duly impressed, and I began to see him. Compared to Allen, Tommy suddenly seemed immature and limited, and so I broke up with him. All through my senior year, I saw Allen, who taught me about Bach, and I taught him about Impressionism. He took me to my senior prom and then he left for Israel, but not until he helped me find the courage to leave Chicago.

I had applied for college and was trying to choose between several schools, among them the University of Chicago, the Art Institute, and the University of California at Los Angeles (UCLA). I don't know what had made me apply to UCLA, probably an unconscious desire to get away from Chicago, but I had decided that, if I received a scholarship to the Art

Institute, I would go there. The scholarship exam was held one Saturday, and the competitors drew and painted all afternoon. After my years of study there, I felt fairly confident that I would receive a scholarship. My drawing satisfied me, but suffered from my usual problem of not being able to fit everything onto the page. I was bitterly disappointed when I did not receive the scholarship, especially when a high school classmate of mine, who did highly illustrative drawings, and who had little serious ambition, informed me that she had received the scholarship that I felt belonged to me. I was awarded a scholarship from my high school, applicable anywhere, and was preparing myself for the scholarship exams for the University of Chicago when the daughter of an old friend of my mother's arrived in Chicago from Los Angeles.

Jessica was two years older than I and positively overwhelmed me with what I saw as her sophistication and worldliness. She was attending UCLA and rapidly convinced me to return to Los Angeles with her. I had been accepted at UCLA, but had lacked the nerve to take the dramatic step of moving twenty-three hundred miles from family and friends, although it was exactly what I needed to do. But Jessica's urging and her descriptions of her Bohemian life provided me with enough support to make the move. I discussed it with my mother, who agreed to let me go, and with Allen, who probably thought that if I was away from home, he could get me to bed, and within three days, packed and left with Jessica on a plane to California.

I moved in with my mother's sister and her husband, a childless couple who lived in Culver City, a squat, desolate part of Los Angeles. My uncle was extremely conservative, and we quickly came to blows. I immediately became involved with the artistic and intellectual circles at the school, joined the NAACP, and before the first semester had elapsed I began seeing a black philosophy student named Leslie. This was the last straw for my uncle, with whom I was now fighting openly. I moved out of my relatives' house and moved in with another art student. I was having a wonderful time, going to folk music concerts, NAACP dances, riding around on the backs of motor scooters, drawing, painting, and doing well in school. My Chicago life seemed a million miles away. I was madly in love with Leslie and imagined him as a black prince. After a while, partly because of pressure from Leslie, I decided to give up my virginity. I was so alienated from my own sexual needs, however, despite my experiences with Tommy, that I dealt with the whole issue intellectually, saying to myself that it was not worth maintaining my virginity if I lost Leslie. To make love because I wanted to was not within my vocabulary.

So Leslie and I decided to have intercourse. Leslie, however, whether due to an aversion to the female genitals or because of misplaced shyness, asked me, at the point of penetration, to put his penis into my vagina. I did not know much about my anatomy, never having masturbated. I tried, but couldn't seem to find the entrance. I fumbled around for a few moments unsuccessfully, until Leslie announced that my inability stemmed from my rejection of him as a black. We argued for some time about this, and finally, our lovemaking unconsummated, fell asleep. The next weekend we tried again, with the same results. Again and again I tried to fit his penis into my vagina, and not knowing how or what it was supposed to feel like, fumbled anxiously around until Leslie would begin, in an accusing voice, to reiterate his theory about the reason for my inability. We never did discuss his not wanting to take the initiative in the situation, and it wasn't until years later that I discovered that he was a virgin, too, and was just as scared and inept as I.

Finally, one night I went into the bathroom with a Tampax and examined myself until I found out how to put it inside my vagina. The next day, I was successful with Leslie, but I remember nothing about the actual act except that for two days afterward, I bled so badly that I had to stay in bed with ice packs on my abdomen. We made love regularly after that, always for about twenty minutes, with Leslie on top. He always used a rubber. I think that I began to have orgasms after a few months, but we never talked about our lovemaking, and Leslie never asked me whether I was enjoying it or if I had come, nor did he ever make any special effort at giving me satisfaction. I assume now that he simply continued until he achieved a climax and, since that took a while, succeeded in giving me some pleasure. Why I was so mad about him, I am not sure, although we had long, philosophical discussions and danced a lot, which I enjoyed. I think there was something about him that reminded me of my father. There was also some strange identification between us.

During the summer after my first year in college, I worked in the art department of a small business. Unexpectedly, Allen came back from Israel and came to L.A. to see me. I was still going with Leslie, and I tried to juggle the two men. One day they even met and talked, but it was very tense. Allen left soon after that meeting, and Leslie and I continued to see each other until the fall, when we broke up at Leslie's insistence, much to my distress.

In the fall of 1958, when school started, I had a new roommate, and I started going with my anthropology teacher. He was short, stocky, and intellectual. I think his name was Scott. We made love five or six times, and it was terrible. Even though Leslie and I had never discussed our lovemaking, I had become accustomed to it lasting for an extended period, at least long enough for me to have an orgasm.

Scott got on top of me, put his penis in me, came, then got
up. He wanted to marry me, but I broke up with him,
feeling repulsed. He didn't understand why I wouldn't marry
him. He thought our relationship of two weeks was terrific.

Some months later, my roommate brought home a tall,
lean, intense-looking fellow named Jerry. We were immediately
attracted to each other, but for some reason I resisted him,
perhaps because I was developing some strange feelings about
men as a result of the experience with Scott and several other
guys with whom I had become involved. Anyway, Jerry and I
knew each other for several months before we began to go
together. Jerry was extremely gifted and completely undirected.
He wandered from job to job, lived on unemployment, borrowed money from his parents, or gambled and won. He was
brilliant and witty and terribly self-destructive, and I tried
again and again during the next two years to break up with
him, but I kept going back. If Leslie bore a vague physical
resemblance to my father, Jerry was his intellectual reflection,
and I couldn't seem to stop myself from becoming involved
with him.

Our early sexual relationship was fair, with Jerry performing strenuously, trying to impress me with his virility. Later,
we developed a constant, though limited rhythm, reaching
mutual orgasm every time we made love. There was, however, great sexual tension between us, and we often rushed
out of restaurants, leaving our dinners half-eaten, tumbling
over each other in our excitement, finally arriving, half un-
dressed, at the apartment we shared, and scrambled into bed.
But we argued frequently, mainly about Jerry's lack of direction. I was a disciplined, hard-working girl, and I resented
his relaxed pace. He often sat around reading, watching TV,
and I guess the resemblance to my father's patterns, much
as they attracted me, also frightened me. It is clear that in

my relationships with men, there was a high component of searching for a father figure with whom I could work out some of the unresolved issues that resulted from my father's death.

At the end of the summer, my mother and brother moved to Los Angeles. But I was not ready to deal with my mother and all the feelings she brought back to me. It was not until I had worked through my past that we could relate again. Jerry and I were almost out of money, as he had not worked for some time, and my income wasn't enough to sustain us. Jerry went gambling, and when he lost our remaining funds, we decided to leave Los Angeles for New York. The logic of this escapes me, but I know it was tied up with my not being ready to face my mother. We hitchhiked across the country, encountering a series of bizarre and frightening men who stopped at the sight of a young couple on the road, an unusual sight in 1959.

We arrived in New York at midnight, riding into the city in the back of a pickup truck, huddled under a tarp to protect ourselves against a gentle rain that stopped as we were crossing the bridge into the city. We lived there for a year, continuing our pattern of breaking up and going back together. By Christmas, I had found a couple of part-time jobs teaching art, and I was enrolled in a painting class, which I soon dropped because the teacher was too conservative. I developed a pattern of painting in the mornings and then, about two in the afternoon, going to work, walking through the streets of the city, absorbing all of its energy. Our friends consisted primarily of people from the Village, most of whom did nothing and proclaimed themselves artists of one sort or another. Many of them were involved with drugs, and a few of the women turned tricks. I experimented a little with drugs, but I was always too frightened to risk doing more than that, preferring my regular work schedule to the artificially induced highs that my friends were experiencing. After a few months, I felt that I had had enough of New York and wanted to go back to Los Angeles and finish my schooling.

In the fall, I flew back alone to Los Angeles and moved into a small house, having broken up with Jerry again. I saw a lot of one of my friends from school, Lloyd, and I became interested in sculpture. I was having a bad time in the painting department, and the sculpture teacher was very encouraging and sympathetic. He used to include pictures of work by women like Louise Nevelson and Lee Bontecou in his photo displays, and I found that very supportive because, in general and much to my shock, girl students weren't taken too seriously in the art department. Not that I let that dampen my determination. I was not aware that there was anything unusual about my continued dedication to becoming an artist. When male students started making comments about my sex, I took them to task and assured them that neither ideas nor art had sex, feeling very confident about myself and my rights. There was no question in my mind but that my work was the most important thing in my life, and I made that clear to any man with whom I became involved. So far, they had all seemed to accept that, or perhaps they were so nonplused by my saying it that they just went along with it.

I had begun to have stomach attacks in New York and had seen several doctors, all of whom dismissed the pains that doubled me up. I never associated these pains with my father's pains, although they were identical. Jerry returned from New York. We had another round and another breakup, and I moved into yet another place, this time a tiny house at the beach. I had a small backyard where I cast concrete sculptures and strung some heavy ropes, and worked on large clay pieces. I had a battery of tests at the UCLA Medical Center, went back with Jerry again, and at Christmastime, had a stomach attack that was so bad that Jerry took me to the UCLA Hospital, where they took one look at me and at my medical records and they hospitalized me for bleeding ulcers. I was so frightened by the experience that when I was released a month later, I went into therapy.

Therapy was an uphill battle that lasted two and a half years. After seven weeks, I began to cry, and the tears brought relief to the bottled-up grief from my father's death, which I had literally turned inward on myself, eating my own stomach away in an effort to become my father and, in that way, keep him alive. As my painful secrets came out, I looked at the stories I had told myself: that I was guilty of my father's death; that my thoughts and wishes had the power to kill; that I had killed my Uncle Harry by kissing him and killed my father by disappointing him or arguing with him. I cried and cried that year and slowly reconstructed my life, which had been torn apart when I was thirteen years old and had remained ripped and bleeding, but completely hidden.

While I was working through my personal problems in therapy, Jerry and I began to struggle with the problems that kept us in the pattern of coming together and then breaking up. I wanted him to become more responsible, to work regularly, to find a direction for his life. He loved me and wanted to make the relationship work and agreed to make changes in himself and his life. We decided to get married, and in the spring of 1961, we did. He went to work and, though we still fought, we began to make some headway in working things out. Jerry had been very alienated as a young man. Bored in high school, he spent his teens in the movies. He had been extremely lonely and once told me that it was better to be alone than to be involved in a relationship that left one lonely. I guess he felt that with me, he could have the kind of relationship that he wanted, and perhaps because of that, he accepted my work and my demand that we divide the household duties. I remember that we argued about housework. One day, Jerry left his socks on the floor, something he had done more than once. I exploded: "What makes you think that because, by a biological accident, I was born with a cunt, I am supposed to pick up your socks?" Jerry looked shocked for a moment, then laughed and admitted that I was right. When our friends came over and saw Jerry cooking or cleaning, it never occurred to me that there was something unusual about that. I just assumed that, since we both worked, we should both clean.

After we were married for about a year, we got a house in Topanga Canyon, one of the lush, mountainous canyons in Los Angeles. I used the garage for my studio and stone-carved in the large area behind the house. I had become a teaching assistant at UCLA in sculpture. Jerry started therapy and went back to school. He had decided he wanted to be a writer, and he was working at it. That year was really good. We had worked out a lot in our relationship and were both doing well in our individual lives.

Then, one Friday night in June, we came home to find our four-month-old Labrador retriever puppy dead on the road, hit by a car. We were very upset, especially Jerry, who always remembered a puppy he had when he was six, which had been hit by a car in front of his eyes. Our dog's death brought the experience back. We buried her behind the house and went to bed and cried together for a long time. For some reason, Cleo's death seemed like an omen.

On Sunday, we went to the beach with some friends in the used car Jerry and I had just bought. We were trying to

get over the depression caused by our dog's death. At the
beach, one of our male friends began to tell me some of his
observations about my marriage. He said that he felt that I
gave Jerry much more than he gave me. I should have
ignored him, but his words touched a chord in me, as I
was beginning to feel that I was always the one who made
the demands for growth in the relationship. That night, I
tried to express my feelings to Jerry, to make him see that he
held himself back emotionally. He became very defensive and
I was unable to make him understand that what I really
wanted was more contact with him. We went to bed with
the feelings between us unresolved.

The next morning, Jerry made a joke before he left for
his therapy appointment, a sure sign that he wasn't too upset
about our fight of the previous evening. He drove off in our
recently purchased pink-and-white Mercury into a day that
was gray and dreary and slightly rainy. He was due back at
eleven o'clock. By noon he had not returned, and I began to
get anxious. I called the doctor's office and was told that
Jerry had not arrived there for his appointment. Two of our
friends had stayed overnight, and they started calling the
police, the sheriff, and the hospital, but with no results. By
one o'clock, with no word from Jerry, I was becoming more
and more frightened. Janice, a friend who lived nearby, had
come over and decided to look around the area, as there
were some very dangerous curves on the road that led to our
house. After several hours, I heard a car drive up. I went
out the front door and saw Janice get out of the car. I saw
her face. She rushed over to me, but I knew what she was
going to say before the words left her mouth. "He's dead,
Judy, Jerry's dead." I screamed: "No, no, no . . ." and
collapsed in her arms. She helped me into the house, where
I began to telephone people, saying the words to try to make

them real. I called Jerry's father. "Ralph," I said, "Jerry's dead. His car went over the cliff." "No, no," I heard him scream over the phone. I called my mother, my friend Lloyd, our friends in New York. Over and over I said it: "Jerry's dead." Everyone came to the house. I just sat there.

Then Janice took me to my mother's. She stayed with me every minute. The next day she took me to see my therapist, who had canceled all of her afternoon appointments in order to give me as much time as I needed. Later, Dr. Sturgeon told me that if I had not worked through my father's death, Jerry's death would have probably caused me to commit suicide. I had realized that my feelings of guilt about my father's death had been based on fantasy, but still I couldn't help feeling guilty about Jerry. Was I to blame? We had had an argument the night before. Perhaps I had made too many demands on him. It was almost ten years to the month since my father had died. Did I kill everyone I loved? "No, no," said my therapist, and so did the voice inside me that had struggled so long with that same guilt. I had not killed my father. I had not killed Jerry. I had told Jerry my feelings, believing that we'd work it out. We don't kill each other like that. In a way, it would have been easier to accept death if I could blame myself. Then it would somehow be within my control. I had to face that it was outside of my control and that was what was so awful.

I went to see Jerry's doctor. He told me that the last two years of Jerry's life were the best he ever had. He told me he thought Jerry's death was an unconscious suicide, that he couldn't face the struggle he would have to undergo in order to make himself healthy. "Nonsense," my therapist said. "His therapist just feels guilty that he couldn't prevent this awful situation. It was an unfamiliar car, a slippery road, a hairpin curve, it could happen to anyone." Despite the assurances of my therapist, a residue of guilt still remained with me. The source of that guilt was in the deeper reasons for my expression of discontent the night before Jerry's death. I was beginning to emerge from the nightmare void of my childhood experience of death. I was beginning to see myself in new ways, to want new things. I guess that I felt that I was beginning to outgrow Jerry. I didn't want that to happen, I wanted him to grow too. When he died, I felt that my need to develop had killed him. Even as I repeated my therapist's words, I heard the secret place inside me saying: "Jerry couldn't keep up with you. If you hadn't wanted more, he would still be alive." That secret place held the voice of death, and I fought for my right to be who I was. *No, no,* something inside me said. You have a right to grow, to demand, to need. I finally saw that it was my own fears that were speaking to me, my own fantasies telling me that there was something wrong with wanting a lot in life; my own feelings that I would be punished for being strong; and my own distortion that Jerry's death was my punishment.

I didn't have a real funeral, more like a wake, where I could see him. Not for me another disappearing act! I *had* to see him. He lay there, in the coffin, so stiff, with makeup on. Why did they put makeup on? To hide something. What? They said he was killed instantly. His chest hit the steering wheel as the car went over the cliff. He was thrown into the air, his shoes came off, he landed at the bottom of the hill, and when Janice found him, he was covered with ants.

After I saw him in his coffin and said goodbye, Janice and I went to the beach. We stood on the sand and I felt the wind on my cheeks. I could hear the waves, and I suddenly knew that I was alone forever, that I could lose the people I loved anytime, any moment, and that the only thing I had in this life was myself. I knew that day about death, but I knew about it in a grown-up way. My father had become my husband, and I had lost them both. Jerry's death gave me my father's death and for a year and a half, I grieved. My friends moved me into a big, green house at the beach, and I turned to my work as my refuge and my salvation and as the one thing in life that I could never lose. I had realized, that afternoon on the beach, that I must build my life on the basis of my own identity, my own work, my own needs, and the only way I could do that was through my art.

2

Making a Professional Life and an Equalized Relationship

After Jerry's death, I worked in my studio constantly, trying to make images out of my feelings. I did drawings that contained shapes tumbling down the page, like Jerry's body falling through the air and down the cliff. I made images of death and resurrection and frozen contact; shapes trying to touch, forever held in the agony of separation. I wasn't always conscious of the meaning of these images, but in the process of struggling to come to terms with my circumstances, I made myself into the artist I was always determined to be. It was in the year and a half after Jerry's death that I learned what it meant to make art seriously. I also began to understand what difficulties I was going to face as an artist because I was a woman.

When I was an undergraduate, I had noticed that most of the serious students were men, and because I wanted to be taken seriously, I sought the friendship of these men. They often told me that I was "different" from other women. I felt a warm glow of pride in my "specialness" and enjoyed the status that I had as the result of being the only woman they took seriously. I can remember the men at school putting other women down, calling them "chicks" and "cunts." Occasionally, I joined in, feeling a little guilty, but wanting to be "in" with them. I didn't understand at the time why other women weren't interested in the things I was, and I slowly and unknowingly began to absorb the culture's contempt for women, rationalizing my own femaleness, as the men did, by the fact that I was somehow "different."

I had had women teachers before I went to college, but at the university, the respected members of the studio faculty were all male. There were two older women teaching in the painting department; however, they were discounted by the male teachers and students. I can remember talking to one of the women and discovering that she was a fascinating person. She had lived a very independent life, had studied with John Dewey and traveled widely. The other female instructor had a collection of women's art that everyone laughed about and that I never made an effort to see. It makes me feel sad to know that I did not pursue relationships with these women because of male peer pressure. But the men didn't respect them, so how could I?

By the time that I entered graduate school, I was becoming more conscious of my situation as a female student. Continuing hostile comments from men and the absence of other serious women combined to make me conclude that *some* men didn't seem to like women who had aspirations as artists. I remember discussing teaching assistantships with my sculpture teacher, commenting that I was afraid that my sex would disqualify me, having heard that the department didn't give teaching assistantships to women. He assured me that, although there was discrimination in the painting department, he did not practice it, and he was sure that I could get an assistantship in sculpture (an unusual event in 1962). As I remember this period of my life, I realize that there was a knowing and a not-knowing going on within me simultaneously. I was coming to recognize that there was a serious gap between the way I saw myself and the way I was seen by the world. At the same time, I tried to deny the significance of that gap, because I did not want to feel how alienated I really was as a woman who took herself seriously. I was having enough trouble, first coping with the struggle to recover from my father's death, and then, after Jerry died, trying to put my life back together.

Fortunately, I had a tendency to pursue my own objectives regardless of the messages I received. This came partly from my irrespressible confidence that whatever I did was "terrific," partly from my drive and determination, and partly as a result of my life experience with my father. I had learned early that the world's perceptions of a person are not necessarily true, so I tended to discount comments and attitudes that conflicted with my own sense of what was right. My self-confidence, combined with the pressure of my personal problems, tended to make me somewhat oblivious to the social pressures in high school and college that came down on the women of my generation.

Several years after I left college, a school friend told me that she and most of the other young women we knew always felt that the discussions that took place in academic classes were intended to be between male faculty and male students. I had always noticed that most of the other female students were quiet in class, but I had no idea why. I know I felt annoyed that other women didn't take an active role in my classes, but I attributed it to the fact that I was "different" and acted as I wished. As we talked, I remembered that, often, when I raised my hand to speak, I wasn't called on right away, but I just figured that the instructor didn't see my hand. So I kept on waving it around until he called on me. It suddenly dawned upon me, in the context of that conversation, that I had simply refused to "read the signs" that pervaded the college atmosphere, signs that told women to be "good girls" and to accept the inevitable second-class status of our sex. Since I never understood this message, I continued to behave in terms of my own self-expectations and according to the standards of equality I had absorbed from my family.

Nonetheless, I couldn't entirely escape the realization that my ambition, aspiration, and dedication was somewhat unusual in women of my generation. But because I always demanded and got a place for myself in my classes, my relationships, and in my work, I was able to separate myself from that social conditioning that prompted other women to relinquish their goals. I had what seemed at the time to be good relationships with some of the male students, but even those ultimately forced me into greater consciousness of my situation as a developing woman artist. One day in 1963, I visited my friend Lloyd Hamrol's studio. We had been close since I was a freshwoman and he a junior in college. We were always drawn together by our mutual interest in art and by some sense of identification with each other. I don't think the issue of my sex ever came up while we were in school together. He accepted me and my level of ambition, which was very much like his own. We used to joke about being Braque and Picasso. We had dated occasionally and Lloyd always wanted to have a serious relationship. But I tended to see him as my "soul mate," which, somehow, in my eyes, precluded the possibility of any romance. Lloyd continued to visit me when I was married to Jerry and stood by me throughout the period surrounding Jerry's death. After Jerry and I had married, Lloyd had become involved with another woman, whom he married. But his marriage was short-lived.

Lloyd and I had not seen each other for a while because he was working on his Master's show. When I went to his studio, I was shocked. He had changed his way of working and had built a series of large sculptures with techniques that I didn't even realize he knew. They were made of plywood and were entirely different from anything he had done before. When I looked at his work, I felt as if a large gulf had opened up between me and my "soul mate." All those years at school together—drawing, taking classes, sharing ideas. Now, he had begun to work in a way that I knew nothing about. And what differentiated us was sex-role conditioning. He, a male, had grown up learning to put things together, use tools, processes, and techniques that were completely outside my cultural orientation as a woman. When he showed the work in a gallery, people continually commented on his good craftsmanship. I didn't even understand why it was the least bit important how one's "craft" was. In fact, someone at school had told Lloyd that he liked the "deliberately uncraftsmanlike approach" in my work, and I had laughed. Later, when Lloyd and I shared a studio, I never could relate to the idea of building something "right," with which he was always concerned. As long as the piece held together, I couldn't see what difference it made if it was "right" or not. The whole idea of artmaking as an involvement with materials, process,

forms, or "craft" was entirely foreign to me. When, in sculpture class, the teacher had given lectures on long, elaborate,
technical processes, I had barely been able to contain my
boredom. My male friends, although as bored as I was, took
voluminuous notes—preparations, I later discovered, for the
time when they would get jobs teaching sculpture and setting
up sculpture shops. No one had ever even suggested to me
that I would have to "make a living," so I was not involved
with "preparing" myself for a job. (I suppose I just assumed
that "somehow I would get along.") Besides, there were certainly no women who ran sculpture departments, at least none
that I knew of, so it seemed clear that the lectures had no
value at all for me.

I was visiting the galleries often by then, and I could see
that *many* people in the art scene were more concerned
with how something was made than with what it meant.
Lloyd's orientation seemed more consistent with the attitudes
of the art scene than mine. It was very confusing to me that
something could be considered "good" just because it was well
made, independent of its meaning. Yet, in the world of art
galleries, museums, and art magazines, there seemed to be a
set of standards by which art was measured that was very different from anything I had ever known, standards that had to
do not only with craft and process, but with "newness," "issues," and the "formal properties of the work," whatever that
meant. Since I wanted to do "important" work, I felt obliged
to internalize these new and foreign standards.

I began to realize that in order to be taken seriously as
an artist, I would have to develop some knowledge of craft,
process, and technique. I felt extremely uncomfortable with
the tools and machines of sculpture, my cultural orientation
as a woman combining with my upbringing, which stressed

the Jewish intellectual's disdain for physical work. But, as I was determined to be taken seriously, I forced myself to learn how to use tools that I had never seen before, much less used. I didn't want to admit that I didn't know the first thing about the mechanical world, because I knew that my "status" in the art department depended upon the fact that I was "different" from other women, who were "weak" or "dumb." I couldn't exhibit either of those traits or I would be just "another cunt." So I pretended to know what I was doing in the shop. Even when I almost lost a breast in the table saw, I wouldn't ask for help. Instead, I just maintained a "brave front" and bumbled my way through the problems.

In my second year in graduate school, I had a confrontation with my male painting instructors. Although I was working in the sculpture department, I was also painting. The work that I did in the summer after Jerry died had led me to a series of paintings on masonite. As I had begun to learn something about tools by then, I built some large panels to paint on. Lloyd's work and success had influenced me and I had copied the symmetrical, frontal format he was using and stuffed all my falling, tumbling shapes into a position of stasis and formal organization. But I was filling the framework with images that came out of my deepest emotions.

The images in the paintings were biomorphic and referred to phalluses, vaginas, testicles, wombs, hearts, ovaries, and other body parts. The first one, "Bigamy," held a double vagina/heart form, with a broken heart below and a frozen phallus above. The subject matter was the double death of my father and husband, and the phallus was stopped in flight and prevented from uniting with the vaginal form by an inert space. Another of the paintings, "Birth," had an abstract body form composed of reproductive parts that hunched over, as in the birth process. The other paintings were similar in imagery, and although abstract, were very graphic in their expression. There was no emphasis on craft in this work, although by that time, my craftsmanship was adequate. Rather, all of the energy was focused on the images, which grew out of direct feeling and were very overt in their femaleness.

When I showed these paintings to the two painting instructors on my thesis committee, they became irate and began to make irrational objections to the work. I didn't understand why they were upset, and obviously neither did they. They threatened to withdraw their support if I continued to make works like these. One sputtered out something about not being able to show the paintings to his family, and they left, leaving me more confused than ever about standards in art. However, I was getting one message loud and clear. I was putting something into my work that wasn't supposed to be there. Thinking about it, I remembered male instructors making comments about some of my earlier works, drawings and sketches that contained references to female anatomy. "Icc-ch," one man had said, "that looks like a womb." Perhaps, I thought, they didn't like work that looked too womanly.

Looking at the work of graduate candidates that the faculty liked, and whose work bore some relation to mine, I could see that it tended to be more abstract and less graphic in its description of emotional or sexual subject matter, like the work at the better galleries around town, which seemed to be more about painting itself and less about any internal or personal reality. I made some pieces in which the subject matter was less obvious, and my teachers were pleased. I became intimidated and began to hide my subject matter from them, trying to find a way to still be involved with my own content without making it so graphic that the male teachers would respond negatively.

Halfway through my last year in graduate school, I became involved with a gallery run by a man named Rolf Nelson. He used to take me to the artists' bar, Barney's Beanery, where all the artists who were considered "important" hung out. They were all men, and they spent most of their time talking about cars, motorcycles, women, and their "joints." I knew nothing about cars or motorcycles, couldn't really join in on their discussions about women, and obviously didn't have a "joint." They made a lot of cracks about my being a woman and repeatedly stated that women couldn't be artists. I was determined to convince them, as I had convinced the men at school, that I was serious. In an effort to be accepted, I began to wear boots and smoke cigars. I went to the motorcycle races and tried to act "tough" whenever I saw them.

By the time I left school, I had incorporated many of the attitudes that had been brought to bear on me and my work, both in school and in the art scene. I had abandoned the paintings that my graduate advisers disliked so intensely, leaving them in a garage to be destroyed. I had begun to compensate for my situation as a woman by trying to continually prove that I was as tough as a man, and I had begun to change my work so that it would be accepted by men. I used to have dreams about being on a battlefield with bullets zinging across the field in front of me. I felt that I had to get across, but I didn't know how, having never been trained for warfare. I was terrified. Finally, an anonymous hand reached out and helped me across the field safely. The dream symbolized my need to learn how to survive in the rough-

and-tumble male world in order to become visible as an artist. I didn't want to run away or hide in a closet, pursuing my work in total privacy and isolation.

After I finished college, I decided to go to auto body school to learn to spray paint, something several of the male artists had discussed doing. I was the only woman among 250 men, all of whom lined up to see me do my final project, which was spraying an old Ford truck with metallic chartreuse paint. I learned quite a bit that was actually beneficial to me as an artist, the most important being an understanding of the role of craft. I had never actually seen artmaking in terms of "making an object," and learning this concept improved my work. The problem was that I had gone there partly to prove something to the male artists. Recently, a male artist told me that he had held me up as an example to his female students, saying: "You see, if you want to be taken seriously, you've really got to dig in there, like Judy." It may be true about digging in there, but it is a shame that I was made to feel that "digging in" could be measured only in terms of "tough talk," spray paint, and motorcycles.

What I have described is a voyage that I was forced to make out of the female world and into the male world where, I was told, "real" art was made. I learned that if I wanted my work to be taken seriously, the work should not reveal its having been made by a woman. One of the best compliments a woman artist could receive then was that "her work looked like it was made by a man." A sculpture like "In My Mother's House," done while I was in graduate school, was smilingly referred to as "one of Judy's cunts" by male artists. (The imagery was obviously feminine and vaginal.) In "Car Hood," which I made at auto body school, the vaginal form, penetrated by a phallic arrow, was mounted on the "masculine" hood of a car, a very clear symbol of my state of mind at this time.

The next few years were confusing to me both in terms of my life as an artist and my relationships with men in the art world. On the one hand, there were men who were very supportive, but not without reservations. One man, an art critic, used to bring me paint and canvas, mention my work occasionally in his articles, and take me out to dinner. But then he would say, in the middle of a discussion, "You know, Judy, you have to decide whether you're going to be a woman or an artist." One time, when I was going to New York, he suggested that I visit a critic friend of his and said that he would mention that I was coming for a visit in his next letter. When I reached the city, I called him and mentioned our mutual friend. He responded warmly and invited me over to his loft. As I climbed the stairs to his upstairs loft, I was very excited at the idea of meeting a man who was so well-known. I imagined him writing an article on my work, introducing me to artists in New York, taking me to galleries and museums. When I walked into his place, I saw a large man, who limped toward me on what appeared to be a wooden leg. He shook my hand and invited me to sit down. We began to talk, and I asked him if he'd like to see slides of my work. He nodded, but as I reached into my purse for a box of slides, I saw him look me up and down, and I suddenly felt very anxious. He barely looked at my slides, and ignoring my attempts to discuss my work with him, began to try to caress me and push me down on the couch. I moved away from him and suggested that we go to dinner. He agreed, but I knew that the evening was ruined and that I had been totally deluded into thinking that this man was interested in anything but a sexual encounter. I never knew whether my friend, the critic, had made him think, in the note that he had written, that he was sending me to see him so that he could get laid or so he could see my work.

After I returned from New York, Lloyd and I became increasingly more involved with each other. After Jerry's death, I had several affairs, all of which depressed me enormously and made me think that I would have to spend the rest of my life alone. The men with whom I became involved either used me sexually, expected me to "take care" of them, were threatened by my work, or, if they could relate to my work, were unable to relate to me personally. Lloyd seemed to be the only man I knew who cared about *me,* who could relate to my work, and who wanted to be involved with me in other ways as well. At the beginning of 1965, we moved into a loft in Pasadena. At that time, we began a slow struggle to build a loving and equalized relationship, in which we could both be ourselves. For the next few years, my energies were divided between my work in the studio and developing a mature relationship with Lloyd.

It was after I left school that my professional life really began. With it came another dose of discrimination, this time worse than before. It seemed that as my work got better, the resistance to acknowledging that a woman could be an artist grew stronger. After we moved to Pasadena, male artists came to visit and made it clear that they were interested in Lloyd, not me. Gallery and museum people refused to see my work, or if they did, ignored it, or at most, gave me an inappropriate or patronizing response. One museum curator dropped by our studio almost every month. One time, Lloyd asked him if he had seen my new work, and when he said "No," suggested that he go into the studio we shared. My piece, which was quite large, was against one wall. As we walked into the room, the curator went over to a sculpture of Lloyd's that he had seen many times and became completely absorbed in looking at it, asking Lloyd if he had changed the color. Embarrassed, Lloyd said "No" and asked him why he wasn't looking at my piece. When the man still refused to turn around, Lloyd covered his sculpture and demanded that the man look at my work. Finally, he looked at it and mumbled something about it being very beautiful. But by this time I was too hurt to respond, and just fled from the studio crying. Later, when the piece was in a show in New York and much acclaimed, this same man went around bragging about how he visited me all the time. Earlier, he had told me that neither he nor his wife wanted much to do with me because I was too "direct."

During the next five years, I was continually made to feel by men in the art world that there was something "wrong" with me. They'd say things like "Gee, Judy, I like your work, but I just can't cut it that you're a woman." Or male artists who lived in the neighborhood would come over and be astonished that I wouldn't cook for them or cater to their needs. I heard stories from people about how someone said that I was a "bitch" or a "castrater," which hurt me deeply. If I showed work and Lloyd didn't, then I was held responsible for his not being shown, and I was accused of having "cut his balls off." The same thing applied if I did a good work and he did a work that wasn't as good as his last piece. It seemed like I couldn't win. But I wouldn't give up. I knew that what I was confronting came out of the fact that I was a woman, but whenever I tried to talk about that openly, I would be put down with statements like, "Come on, Judy, the suffrage movement is over," and treated as if I were a leper.

All through this period, I worked and I showed my work in

galleries and museums. The two people who helped me most were my dealer and Lloyd; they supported me and stood up for me. My earlier naïveté about my situation as a woman artist was giving way to a clear understanding that my career was going to be a long, hard struggle. Fortunately, I knew that I was okay—that the problem was in the culture and not in me, but it still hurt. And I still felt that I had to hide my womanliness and be tough in both my personality and my work. My imagery was becoming increasingly more "neutralized." I began to work with formal rather than symbolic issues. But I was never interested in "formal issues" as such. Rather, they were something that my content had to be hidden behind in order for my work to be taken seriously. Because of this duplicity, there always appeared to be something "not quite right" about my pieces according to the prevailing aesthetic. It was not that my work was false. It was rather that I was caught in a bind. In order to be myself, I had to express those things that were most real to me, and those included the struggles I was having as a woman, both personally and professionally. At the same time, if I wanted to be taken seriously as an artist, I had to suppress anything in my work that would mark it as having been made by a woman. I was trying to find a way to be myself, still function within the framework of the art community, and be recognized as an artist. This required focusing upon issues that were essentially derived from what men had designated as being important, while still trying to make my own way. However, I certainly do not wish to repudiate the work that I made in this period, because much of it was good work within the confines of what was permissible.

By 1966, I had had a one-woman show, had been in several group and museum shows, and had made a lot of work that could be classified as "minimal," although hidden behind that facade were a whole series of concerns that I did not know how to deal with openly without "blowing my cover," as it were, and revealing that I was, in fact, a woman with a different point of view from my male contemporaries. At that time, I firmly believed that if my difference from men were exposed, I would be rejected, just as I had been in school. It was only by being different from women and like men that I seemed to stand a chance of succeeding as an artist. There was beginning to be a lot of rhetoric in the art world then to the effect that sex had little to do with art, and if you were good, you could make it.

Lloyd had moved into another studio on the same street, leaving me with a five thousand-square-foot studio to myself. He and I had been having a lot of trouble working together, and we decided it would be better if we each had our own place. This need was particularly strong in me because I felt that if people came to my loft and I was alone, they would be less apt to see me in relation to Lloyd. I felt convinced that the only way to make any progress in the art world was to stay unmarried, without children, live in a large loft, and present myself in such a way that I would *have* to be taken seriously.

In 1967, I was working on a piece for a big sculpture show. The piece was called "Ten Part Cylinder" and was made from the forms in which freeway pillars are cast. I needed a large amount of money to finish the piece, and a collector friend of mine introduced me to a man who, he said, was interested in helping me. This man owned a large company that dealt in plastics, and I thought his involvement in plastics was the reason for his interest in my sculpture, which was to be finished with Fiberglas. We went to lunch, and at lunch I discovered the real reason for his offered help. He felt that women "needed help" from men because they were inferior, and he "liked to help women." He went on to say that if a male artist were to ask him for help, it would be very degrading to the artist, and he would refuse, because "men should take care of themselves."

I can remember my throat constricting and my stomach becoming tight. On the one hand, this man was willing to give me all the money I needed to finish my piece, but it meant that I would have to live with the fact that I accepted help from a person who considered me inferior and was only helping me as a way of proving that inferiority since, by accepting the money, I would be reinforcing his belief. I felt a painful and familiar conflict.

Perhaps today I would tell him off and walk out. Then, because I had accepted the idea that I had to be "tough enough" to do whatever I had to in order to get my work done, I accepted his offer, feeling terrible about it. Was it any wonder that in my work I was trying to move as far away as possible from revealing that I was a woman? Being a woman and being an artist spelled only one thing: pain.

Although I was struggling to deny anything in my work that could mark me as a woman, some aspects of my femaleness were intrinsically involved with both my day-to-day activity as an artist and in my developing aesthetic. In fighting for my rights in the art world I was acting out of a feminist consciousness before I knew what to call my point of view. When I worked in my studio I came into contact with those areas of my personality structure that had been crippled by female role conditioning. This was particularly true in relation to my expectations of the male art authorities, who I tended to see as a child sees a parent. I kept expecting to gain approval from them, particularly since I had grown up expecting to be loved for whatever I did. It was a continual shock to me to discover that instead of love and approval, I encountered hostility and rejection. Now it is clear to me that to expect men to validate one for challenging male dominance (which is what a woman artist implicitly does, simply by being a woman and an artist) is entirely fantastic. But, at the time, I kept going out into the world with my vulnerability and my need for love and acceptance, only to slowly and painfully realize that I had to change my expectations. Instead of looking to the male world to approve of me and my work, I had to learn to approve of myself and to see myself, not as a child to be approved of by someone "out there," but rather as a creator with something to give to the world. In some strange way, the rejection I faced strengthened me, but only because it forced me to learn to live on my own hook, to use *my* values, instincts, and judgments as my guides.

My work itself reflected my struggles, albeit indirectly. The hard materials (plastics and metals), perfect finishes, and minimal forms in my work of 1966 and 1967 were "containers" for my hidden feelings, which flashed in the polished surfaces, shone in the light reflections, and disappeared in the mirrored bases. I had entirely stopped painting by 1965 and was making sculpture. My pieces were either very small and rearrangeable, which made the viewer huge in relation to them, or were large, simple pieces that one walked through and was dwarfed by. This duality paralleled my own experience: In my studio, I was large and able to manipulate my own circumstances; in the world, I was small and could get lost in values and attitudes that were hostile and foreign to me. The small, rearrangeable pieces had another dimension that was directly related to the struggles Lloyd and

I were going through in trying to be independent while still maintaining a close relationship.

By 1967, Lloyd had gotten a teaching job in San Diego and was away three days a week. This forced us both to take more responsibility for our respective lives and not depend so much upon each other to "fill in" the gaps and spaces. During his absence, I lived my life in terms of my own needs, but as soon as he returned, I "put down" my life and began to rearrange my schedule to suit him. This reflected the fact that I felt that his needs were more important than mine and also that I still assumed that my life should be open-ended to accommodate his demands. Although I had been able to assert my own identity in the obvious areas of my life—housework, sex, my work—in the more subtle areas, I found myself face to face with many problems that grew out of role conditioning.

I dealt with most of these *through* my work. In going to auto body school, learning to use tools and machines, facing and overcoming rejection and difficulties in the world, working on large-scale pieces, I was moving out of the limits of female role, which was healthy. Although aspects of my work process were shaped by male pressure, my own desire to grow and be a whole and functioning artist also motivated me. When I made the small, rearrangeable pieces and the large sculptures through which one walked, I was trying to give voice to my own feelings of "moving through" and "out into" an unfamiliar world, trying to gain control over my life, trying to expand my capacities. One might almost say that the years 1965–67 were spent exploring those aspects of my personality that this culture calls masculine: my strength, both physical and mental, my assertiveness, my ability to conceptualize. It is interesting that it was during this period that I encountered hostile statements to the effect that I was trying to be a man and that I was "castrating" Lloyd.

If I as a woman was seen stereotypically during this period, my relationship with Lloyd was utterly incomprehensible to the people around us, and to some extent this is still true. From the time I first met him, when I was eighteen and he was twenty, he loved me and I cared for him, but I hadn't been able to accept him for a long time because he didn't fit male stereotypes any more than I fit female ones. To the degree that I acted in typically unfemale ways, he acted in ways that were similarly nonmale. As I was able to be assertive and ambitious, he was able to be supportive and noncompetitive, which was harder for me to accept because aspiring toward "masculine" standards when you are a woman has more status than demanding that you have the right to be "feminine" if you are a man. Though neither of us could fit into the narrow confines of role expectation, both of us had absorbed some of the cultural attitudes that there was something "wrong with us" because of that. We both knew that the standard male-female relationship as it existed in the society could not contain our personalities. Even my relationship with Jerry (as it had been) was not developed enough to accommodate me at that point in my growth, so it could not serve as a model for us. Lloyd and I had to struggle together to make a relationship that could allow us *both* to realize our personal ambitions. I think we had shied away from that difficult task for a long time and had avoided becoming involved with one another until we both had developed to the point that we could take on a struggle to make an equalized relationship at a time in history when there was no support for such an effort.

When we first got together, at the end of 1964, we cried with relief, feeling, as we made love, that we were looking at our own reflection in the face of another person and that we were finally able to acknowledge our feelings for each other. In our struggle to emerge from the layers of role conditioning we each still suffered from, we fought, screamed, cried, punched each other, took our frustrations out on each other, pushed each other into increasingly greater independence, supported each other's desires to grow, to risk, and to change. Lloyd went into extended therapy in order to peel away the defenses he had developed, which were causing him great pain. Often, it was he more than I who hung on in the relationship when it looked as if there were no hope.

We never had any problems about housework. Lloyd simply assumed that he would do half and, because I was by that time, threatened by "female chores," sometimes he did more than half. During the Pasadena years, Lloyd was often torn between his feelings for me and his own needs for recognition, because male art establishment visitors liked to extol him while putting me down. It was as if people could not imagine that it was possible for two talented people, one a man, the other a woman, to be interdependent and supportive. They seemed to want to distort our relationship so that it fit the stereotype of the talented man and his female follower, or the strong woman and her castrated boyfriend. All through those years, everyone put us down, and we had only each other to hold on to, somehow feeling that verifying ourselves in each other's eyes helped us both stand up to society's stereotypical methods of dealing with an untypical couple.

When Lloyd and I had been together about a year, he began therapy. He saw a male psychiatrist, who, after several months, asked Lloyd to bring me to a session. Apparently, he, like some other people we knew, had decided that Lloyd's problems were caused by me, that my strength was making him weak. When we went to the office, the therapist began to attack me, looking at Lloyd as if to say: You see, she's not so tough. Just put her down like this, then you'll be strong and she'll be weak. The man really took me apart. Lloyd sat silent, in agonized distress. At that point in his life, it was very difficult for him to express his feelings. All he could do was to internalize them and suffer. When we went home, I went to bed for twenty-four hours, trying to examine, evaluate, and recover from the things the doctor had said. I knew that the way he saw me and our relationship was entirely different from how I saw myself and my relationship with Lloyd. I finally had to conclude that the man was projecting social stereotypes onto us, and the next week, when we went back to his office, I tried to tell him that. My efforts enraged him, and he began to attack me again. No matter what I said, the man just kept telling me that I was wrong. Finally, I broke down, became hysterical, and we went home. Lloyd still had not been able to stand up to him, but he never really communicated with him again. He just withdrew into a hostile silence for the remaining months of his treatment, which made his therapist continually ask him whether he thought the therapy was a failure. Lloyd may not have been able to challenge the doctor's sexist assumptions that his weakness was a result of my strength, but deep down inside himself, Lloyd knew that I was his friend, that I had been his friend for years, and that I was probably the only person in the world who really was his friend.

Lloyd and I used to get into these long emotional struggles, which went on endlessly without resolution. Because he had difficulty expressing his feelings, he would often be unable to explain to me what was going on with him. For example, if he did something that hurt me, I would tell him how badly he had made me feel and ask him why he had said such a thing. Instead of just telling me that he felt badly about hurting me, he would become defensive, tell me that I shouldn't feel like that, and then withdraw, I would become frantic, demanding that he deal with the situation. The more I insisted, the more he withdrew. Then I would begin to yell at him, taking out a lot of my own personal frustrations on him. Soon he'd be yelling back, saying irrational things, throwing things, punching walls, trying to release his pent-up and unexpressed feelings. Sometimes these scenes would go on all day, with no resolution. Then we would have to separate. Lloyd would go up the street to his studio and I wouldn't hear from him for days on end.

At other times, Lloyd would want to spend time with me and not be able to tell me that he needed me. Instead, he would say something nasty to me. Then he'd leave, getting into the car and driving off without telling me where he was going or when he'd be back, knowing that his action would stimulate all of my abandonment anxieties. After Jerry's death, I was always afraid that something terrible would take place again. If Lloyd was ten minutes late coming home, he would find me hysterical, terrified that something had happened to him. My vulnerability in this area allowed Lloyd an easy target. If he wanted to make himself feel like he was a "bad guy," he would come home late, leave me when I needed him, or not call me to tell me where he was. It took a long time for *both* of us to take responsibility in this area; he by not taking advantage of my weakness, and I by not expecting him to compensate for the pain my life experiences had left me with. Finally, I began to trust that Lloyd *would* come home safely, although even now I get edgy when he is late, and I always look up and down the alley when I drive home to make sure that one of our cats is not lying there, dead.

Lloyd continued therapy, this time with a woman. He made a lot of progress with her, and our relationship improved. I began to learn how to accept his difficulty in expressing his feelings exactly at the moment he felt them. Instead of getting angry at him, I learned to recognize that I wasn't going to get the satisfaction I needed at the moment, trust that Lloyd would tell me his feelings later, and force myself to go into my studio and do my work. My friend Janice helped me through this period by supporting me for not using my energy struggling with Lloyd, but rather recognizing when something couldn't be resolved and continuing on my own track. My learning to do this also aided Lloyd, as he was able to realize that it wasn't so terrible if he couldn't always come through. He tended to punish himself for days after one of our scenes, feeling like he had failed me.

In therapy, he came in contact with years of repressed anger, which he had only been able to express in self-destructive ways: breaking his own hand against a fence in a fit of rage, kicking holes in doors, or smashing windows. This anger grew out of his feeling that he had to perform as a "nice guy" in the world, the male role he felt compelled by his upbringing to play. The struggle with his rage culminated when I went to visit him one time in San Diego. We had a real knock-down, drag-out fight while we were driving in the car. At one point, Lloyd was trembling with fury and, stopping the car, he screamed at me, threatening to throw me out, to kill me. He shouted that he hated me; he was almost purple with wrath. After this explosion, he calmed down and we both realized that he had seen the limit of his anger and felt less terrified of it. His fantasy had been that if he allowed himself to express those feelings, he would actually kill me or himself. Well, he *had* expressed them, and nothing horrible had happened. That evening marked a real turning point in our relationship.

Sex posed another area of difficulty for us. I did not know how to express my needs directly and specifically. I only knew how to say "I need," expecting Lloyd to somehow miraculously figure out how to give me what I needed. When I projected that expectation, he would freak out, feeling that he would be subsumed and devoured by my need. One day, instead of just expressing my usual generalized neediness, I asked Lloyd to do something specific. We were making love, and I had had one orgasm. I needed another one, and I asked him to move in a special way. It was amazing. He looked at me and said, "That's easy, I can do that." He had never been able to give me more than one orgasm easily, as he often felt threatened by the fact that I wasn't finished when he was. By expressing my needs clearly, he could see that my needs had a limit and that I didn't expect him to "perform forever." This allowed him to relax, respond to my need, and fulfill it. After that day, many of our sexual problems subsided.

As Lloyd and I worked on our relationship, I began to come increasingly in touch with the nature of my sexuality, both through our struggles and in my work. I had spent several years trying to move away from identifying as a woman, and as long as I was inside of my studio working, I could see myself as a "person." Because Lloyd and I were living separately, I had to learn to become more independent. As I did this, I came more in contact with myself and my needs. But, as I became more able to express those needs in my life and in my work, I began to feel more and more alienated from the society.

I might be a "person" inside my loft, but if I walked half a block away from my studio, some man would make a pass at me or I would go by a nudie bookstore, with the bodies of women displayed for all to see. I couldn't go to a movie without encountering the most distorted female characters, women who didn't bear any resemblance to this "person" I felt myself to be. Everywhere I went I had to endure the same kind of distorted attitudes toward women, and the more I experienced myself as a "person" in my studio, the more unbearable it became to realize that I was being treated as a "woman" in the world. I had come to realize that when I showed a male artist or curator my work, his perceptions were filtered through his attitudes toward women. So by 1968, I had ceased showing my work to many people, had become particular about where and under what circumstances I would show, and was living in virtual isolation. I wasn't even seeing Lloyd too often, because he was in a period during which he had broken down many of his destructive behavior patterns but had not yet succeeded in replacing them with new and healthier ones. So we had decided to confine our time together to those moments when he felt he could act positively, out of his caring for me.

I could no longer pretend in my art that being a woman had no meaning in my life; my entire experience was being shaped by it. I decided to try and deal with it in my work, to symbolize my sense of myself. I also wanted to explore the nature of my sexuality. Having been brought up with 1950s sexual mores, I had been taught that mutual orgasm was the ultimate in sexual satisfaction. It had been continually puzzling to me why, after Lloyd and I had come together, I was still unsatisfied. I had felt that there must be something wrong with me, until I stumbled on that method of expressing my needs clearly, which allowed me to get what I needed. Then I began to realize that my real sexual identity had been denied by my culture, and this somehow represented the entire sense of denial I had been experiencing as a woman artist. I felt that if I could symbolize my true sexual nature, I could open up the issue of the nature of my identity as a woman through that symbolic statement.

As I was still trying to "slip by" in the male world and express myself without losing validation from men, I decided to use three dome shapes, the simplest forms that I could think of that had reference to my own body, breasts, fecundity, while maintaining the necessary neutrality for the art world. Each of the three domes were made of a transparent material and had layers inside that could not be clearly seen, an interesting metaphor for my own hidden depths. The layers were sprayed with softly changing colors, which overlapped and overlayed inside the forms. In order to make these pieces, I had to slowly and painstakingly develop technical skills. I had not sprayed since auto body school, and now I wanted to spray on plastic, which was difficult to do and which no one on the West Coast had yet done, certainly not in the scale that I ultimately used. I began making some tests and working on color systems that would make the forms feel as if they were dissolving. I was trying to invent a format for expressing what it was like to be female and to have a multi-orgasmic sexuality (this was before the Masters and Johnson studies were published). Along with trying to begin dealing with issues about the nature of my identity as a woman, I was involved with the final resolution of my family relationships. I still had an unresolved sense of loss and an unclear self-image. The dome shapes stood for the essential family unit of mother, father, and child as well as my multiple sexuality. One could walk around the domes and see them from all sides, which allowed them to be examined for their constantly changing relationships. I often think now about the contained quality of the color in the domes, the way it was trapped inside the swollen breast of belly form. Also, the fact that so much subject matter was hidden in such simple shapes is a testament to the gap that existed between my real concerns as a woman and the forms that the professional art community allowed a "serious" artist to use.

Even though I neutralized the subject matter of this work, I was identified as revealing my femaleness when a woman artist from New York came to my studio with the director of a local museum. She looked at the domes and remarked scornfully, "Ah, the Venus of Willendorf," a reference to early female fetishes. I was devastated. It was one thing to approach issues about my own femaleness, no matter how indirectly. It was quite another to be identified as doing so. Again, my femaleness was creeping into my work, as it had done in graduate school, and again it was being rejected, this time by a woman. After a while, I recovered from my distress and realized that whether my work would be accepted or not, I *had* to work through these issues. After all, on one level, I *was* the Venus of Willendorf and all that she symbolized. Rather than running away, I would have to find a way to affirm myself and my own identity as a woman artist. But could I do that and still maintain my status as "an artist of the world"? I did not want to relinquish the professional identity I had fought so hard to secure.

3

Back to Painting/
Getting Married/
The Women's Movement

The domes led me back to painting. I began working on a series of images of small sheets of clear acrylic, spraying them with an air brush and using them as models for the color layouts in the domes. Then I became interested in the two-dimensional forms independent from the domes. I felt I could use a flat format better than a sculptural one for the issues I was dealing with. One thing two-dimension afforded was a body identification between myself and the painted forms. This was hard to achieve in sculpture, which seemed to exist outside of oneself so much more. At first, the forms—three round shapes, one above the other two—were blobby, undefined, as if to say that my own self-image was still undefined. Then I did some drawings in which the centers of the forms were dark. I felt the darkness in my stomach as a sense of wrongness, as if there were something wrong with *me,* and I knew

that I was going into the place inside me that had been made
to feel wrong by my experiences in the male-dominated world.
I opened the forms and let them stand for my body experience
instead of my internalized shame. The closed forms transmuted
into doughnuts, stars, revolving mounds, which represented
cunts. (I use that word deliberately, as it is that word that
most embodies society's contempt for women. In turning the
word around, I hope to turn society's definition of the female around and make it positive, instead of negative, at least
in my work.) I chose that format because I wanted to express
what it was like to be organized around a central core, my
vagina, that which made me a woman. I was interested in a
dissolving sensation, like one experiences in orgasm. It seemed
to me that my experience as a woman had a dual nature. On
the one hand, it was through my cunt that I made contact
with Lloyd, who affirmed me and gave me great pleasure, especially at the moment of orgasm, when I was totally vulnerable and exposed and loved for being in that state. At the same
time, because I had a cunt, I was despised by society. By
making an image of the sensation of orgasm, I was trying to
affirm the fact of being female and thus implicitly challenge
male superiority.

I made shapes where the central holes contracted and expanded, clicked around in a circle, twisted, turned, dissolved,
thrust forward, and became soft, both consecutively and
simultaneously. I repeated the forms in an effort to establish
a continuum of sensation. As I went along, the paintings
became increasingly difficult technically. But that difficulty
seemed to be a parallel to the emotional risk they represented
for me. The color systems I had been developing allowed me
to establish a method of representing emotional states through
color—thus assertiveness could be represented by harsh colors,

receptiveness through softer, swirling color, the state of orgasm through color that dissolved. I began to combine these various color systems with the forms I was evolving in order to try to convey the multiple aspects of my own personality and thus assert the fullness of the female self as I experienced it. Again, I was working within a male-oriented form language, which inherently limited the degree to which all this information could be seen, but I did not appreciate this at the time.

In 1969, I began a series of paintings entitled "Pasadena Lifesavers." They embodied all of the work I had been doing in the past year, reflecting the range of my own sexuality and identity, as symbolized through form and color, albeit in a neutralized format. There were fifteen paintings, five feet by five feet, sprayed on the back of clear acrylic sheets, then framed with a sheet of white Plexiglas behind the clear sheet. The series consisted of five images, painted in three different color series. The first series was hinged on red/green opposition, a combination that caused the forms to gray out. I was frightened by the images, by their strength, their aggressiveness. I had internalized parts of society's dictum that women should not be aggressive, and when I expressed that aspect of myself through forms that were quite assertive, I became frightened and thought there was "something wrong with the paintings." Lloyd helped me then, as he had so many times, making me see that there was nothing wrong with my aggressiveness. As I recovered from my feelings of shame for having revealed something that was so different from the prevailing concepts of "femininity," I gradually accepted the paintings, and in so doing, also accepted myself more fully.

The next group was softer; the paintings were based on what I called spectral color—that is, starting with one color and moving on to one close to that color in the spectrum until

I arrived back at the beginning color. The images and ground interplayed as I carried over the segments of color into the background, which I had not done in the first group. The third series was blue-green-purple in color and bleached out when looked at for any length of time. As I think of the "Pasadena Lifesavers" now, I can see the three groups as representing my "masculine" aggressive side, my "feminine" receptive side, and the hiding of myself that I was still doing at the time. But the paintings function on many levels and, as well as possessing layers of symbolic meanings, which can be read if one knows how to read abstract form, they are also visually engaging. They were a first step in my struggle to bring together my point of view as a woman with a visual form language that allows for transformation and multiple connotations.

While I worked on "Pasadena Lifesavers," I also executed a series of smoke pieces in which the color inside the domes and the paintings was freed from the rigid structures in which it had been imprisoned and allowed to gush into the air. The "atmospheres" reflected the release that I felt as a result of making these paintings. Through the "Pasadena Lifesavers," I was able to emerge from the many constraints of role conditioning, for as I symbolized the various emotional states that comprised my personality, I gave myself permission to experience and express more aspects of myself. When I finished the paintings, I felt like icebergs were breaking up inside me. By making images of my feelings, I was able to liberate myself from the guilt about my needs, my aggressiveness, my power as a person. However, although I was feeling increasingly liberated as a person and a woman within my artistic and personal life, I was still discovering that this liberation did not necessarily extend to the outside world.

When I was working on the "atmospheres," I became involved with the only fireworks company on the West Coast capable of producing the smoke devices I needed. The company, located near San Bernardino, was run by a man who, like other men in the business world, was intrigued by the idea of a woman entering a male preserve. At first, he was very nice, although he occasionally made sexist cracks, which I tried to ignore. In order to be in control of the process of setting off the smoke devices, I decided to become a pyrotechnician. To do this, it was necessary for me to "shoot" three fireworks shows. As there were few female pyrotechnicians, I needed the support of the fireworks company, not only for the production of the material, but also for show dates, help with the state tests, and authorization for buying and detonating the smoke devices.

All went well during the year I was ordering materials and doing my pieces around California. I fended off the fireworks guy, ignoring his gradually more insistent remarks about women, sex, and me. Finally, when I was in San Diego to shoot a July 4 show in the stadium, the man became entirely impossible to deal with. We were both staying down there, and he kept trying to get me to go to his motel after we finished working. I resisted, and at one point, he threw himself down on the grass and began humping the ground, saying, "I could do it to you right here." Then he got up and began rubbing himself against me. I kept trying to push him away. After about ten minutes of his alternately humping the grass and rubbing against me, he gave up, but not until he had made me feel like I never wanted to go near him again.

After this experience, I did something I had never done before: I gave up something I wanted to do. I stopped studying to become a pyrotechnician and I didn't do another "Atmos-

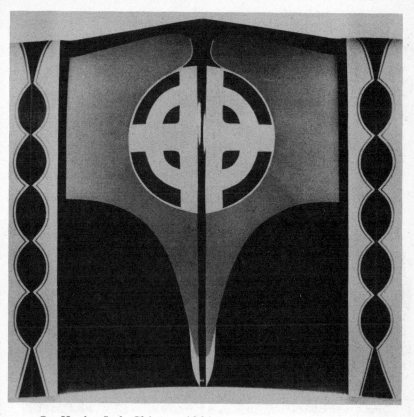

Car Hood, © Judy Chicago, 1964;
sprayed acrylic lacquer on Chevrolet hood, 4' x 6'
(Collection: Mr. and Mrs. Radoslar L. Sutnar, Los Angeles, CA. Photo
courtesy Through the Flower Archives)

This image perfectly symbolizes the conflict between my personal subject matter, which concerned my experiences as a
young woman, and the visual forms that were acceptable in
the Los Angeles art scene during the sixties.

Untitled Painting, © Judy Chicago, 1964;
sprayed acrylic on canvas, 4' x 4' (Collection: Marion Sampler,
Los Angeles, CA. Photo courtesy Through the Flower Archives)

After graduate school, I buried what remained of my personal content in a severe abstract style.

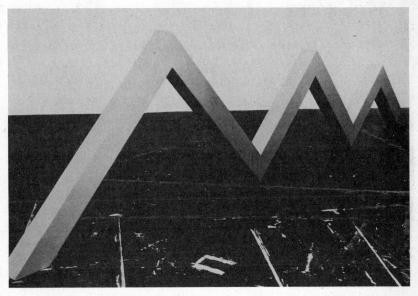

ZigZag, © Judy Chicago, 1965;
acrylic, canvas, and wood, 20' x 6' (destroyed) (Photo courtesy
Through the Flower Archives)

This is an example of my efforts at the Minimal art style popular
during the sixties. I had "gotten the message" that I couldn't be
a woman and an artist too, at least not in my imagery.

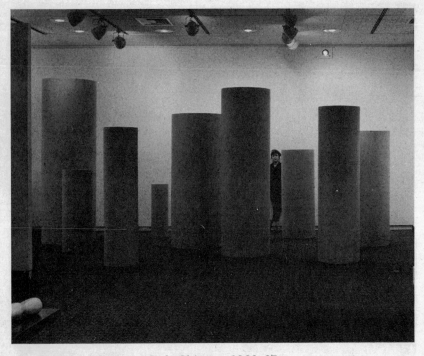

Ten Part Cylinders, © Judy Chicago, 1966–67;
Fiberglas, 20' x 20' installed (destroyed)
(Photo courtesy Through the Flower Archives)

I spent months executing this piece for the *Sculpture of the Sixties* exhibition for the Los Angeles County Museum of Art, working at a boat-works company learning to handle Fiberglas. Shortly before I completed it, I ran out of funds. A friend of mine introduced me to a potential funder who said that, had I been a man, he would have thought it degrading that I had asked for money. But since I was female, he thought it was okay and he agreed to give it to me. I felt humiliated; I was caught in a conflict between my desire to finish the sculpture in order to be in an important show and my pride as a woman. I decided to take the money, but I never forgot the incident.

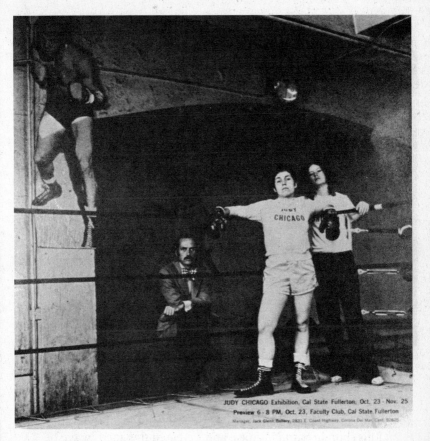

JUDY CHICAGO Exhibition, Cal State Fullerton, Oct. 23 - Nov. 25
Preview 6 - 8 PM, Oct. 23, Faculty Club, Cal State Fullerton
Manager, Jack Glenn Gallery, 2821 E. Coast Highway, Corona Del Mar, Calif. 92625

Exhibition announcement, 1971
(Photo courtesy Through the Flower Archives)

This announcement was sent out by the Jack Glenn Gallery
and then published in *Art forum* in 1971. Throughout the seventies, I would see the image posted in women artists' studios
around the country, and for years, male artists asked me if I
wanted to box. Though I had intended it as a satiric comment
on the macho ads of my male artist friends in Los Angeles, it
obviously embodied the fact that in the early seventies women
artists "came out fighting."

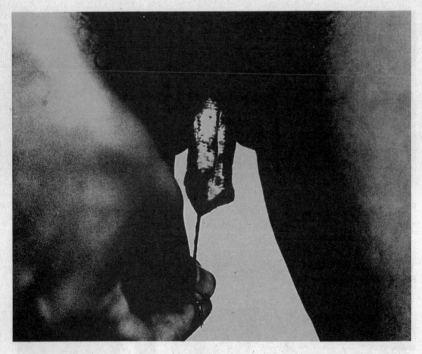

Red Flag, © Judy Chicago, 1971;
photo-lithograph on paper, 20" x 24"
(Photo: Donald Woodman)

In 1971, the artist Sam Francis invited me to do a lithograph
at his shop in Santa Monica, and I created this early image of
menstruation. When I showed a slide at the first West Coast
women's art conference (which Miriam Schapiro and I organized at Cal Arts), women in the audience began screaming
at me, accusing me of having created an image of a "bloody
penis." I was shocked that they were unable to identify the
image, which proves my comment in the Preface that "what is
not imaged does not exist." In other words, because women
have been deprived of visual images that affirm our experiences, they were unable to recognize the visual record of an
act they perform monthly.

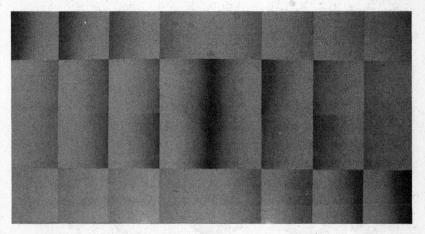

Desert Fan, © Judy Chicago, 1971;
sprayed acrylic on sheet acrylic, 5' x 10'
(Collection: Mary Ross Taylor, Houston, TX. Photo courtesy Through
the Flower Archives)

In 1971, at the same time that I was starting to "come out"
with my real content, I was also struggling to integrate it with
the formal artmaking structure I had developed. My goal was
to fuse my personal subject matter with the transformed
visual forms of contemporary art.

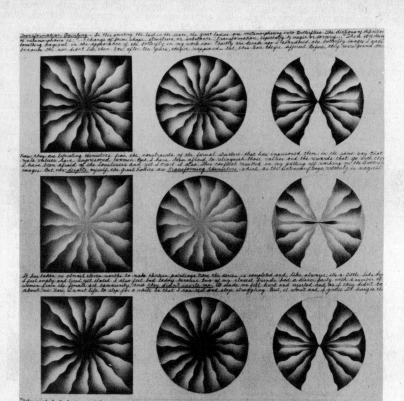

Great Ladies Transforming Themselves into Butterflies,
© Judy Chicago, 1973;
sprayed acrylic on canvas, 40" x 40"
(Collection: Deborah Marrow and Michael McGuire, California.
Photo courtesy Through the Flower Archives)

In 1973, I began to add writing to my paintings in an effort to
make my visual intentions clear. At the time, I didn't know
how to use my abstract form language in a way that allowed
the content to be clearly understandable to my audience,
which was already becoming wider and more diverse. I also
began to reintegrate the butterfly image that had appeared
in my earlier work and which, I learned, was an ancient
symbol of both the Goddess and of liberation.

phere" for several years. Occasionally, someone from out of Los Angeles saw the slides of the smoke pieces and asked me if I'd be interested in doing one. I always hemmed and hawed and slid out of the question because I was too embarrassed to say that I stopped doing them because I couldn't deal with this man who ran the fireworks company. Finally, I met a woman who had succeeded in becoming a pyrotechnician and this encouraged me to resume working with fireworks.

In thinking about this, I realize that I couldn't cope with the situation because it indicated that I was "failing" in my attempts to be an "artist" in the world and I couldn't stand to see myself as a "failure." I had always managed to "slip by" —to be different from other women. I guess it was only a matter of time until I came up against a situation that was too much for me. After that scene in San Diego, I retreated still farther into my studio. I tried to pursue my work the best I could. Then, the first material from the slowly developing women's movement reached the West Coast. When I read it, I couldn't believe it. Here were women saying the things I had been feeling, saying them out loud. I trembled when I read them, remembering the put-downs I encountered whenever I had tried to express the facts of my life as a woman artist. I had so internalized the taboo about mentioning it that I shuddered with terror reading Valerie Solanas' book and some of the early journals of the women's movement. Even though I thought Solanas extreme, I recognized the truth of many of her observations, and I identified with all the material in those early tracts as I had never identified with anything in my whole life.

As I read, I slowly allowed the information to seep into my pores, realizing that at last there was an alternative to the isolation, the silence, the repressed anger, the rejection, the depreciation, and the denial I had been facing. If these women could say how they felt, so could I. Coincidentally, I had been invited by several colleges in the area to speak about my work. I decided to use the opportunities to express my real feelings, to reveal what I had been going through as a woman and an artist. I was so scared. My voice shook, I could hardly talk. I spoke about the isolation and the rejection, the put-downs and the distortions. I spoke about my anger toward men because they had used me sexually. Everyone was shocked; there were angry reactions from the men. I drove home and trembled in terror at the fantasies that told me that something terrible was going to happen because I was saying the unsayable. I was telling the truth about my experiences as a woman, and I felt sure that I would be punished for it, that someone would break into my studio and destroy all my paintings or would shoot me or beat me up.

For one entire year, I lived in terror. I recognized that my fear reflected how deeply I had internalized society's taboos about revealing my real feelings. I had been told that if I told men the truth, I would "castrate" them, and I was afraid that they would retaliate. But I felt that I *had* to reach out and take this opportunity to be myself, offered implicitly by the women's movement. I accepted the fear as part of my day-to-day experience and just felt it every day, every time I attempted to reveal my own point of view. Even now, five years later, each time I make another step in exposing my real feelings, the fears engulf me again. The difference is that I have tangible support from women now; then I was alone and had only a few books to tell me that there were other women who were also speaking out.

Throughout this period, the only person I had to depend on was Lloyd. Even though he himself was trapped in the role of "nice guy" and was often unable to express his real feelings, he identified with my struggle and supported me every step of the way, even when my growth made him feel threatened. By the beginning of 1969, we had worked through many of the problems that had prevented us from realizing the relationship that we both wanted—one that allowed us to be ourselves, to realize our personal ambitions and to be able to relate easily and directly. After the big scene in San Diego, things had calmed down considerably between us. Lloyd's therapy was beginning to pay off, and he was establishing new and healthier behavior patterns. I was becoming more independent and self-sufficient. In the spring of 1969, we decided to get married, probably as a way of affirming the relationship we were making, which was so untypical in so many ways that we both felt the need to give it *some* shape that related to social mores. Also, after having experienced the destruction of my first marriage, I needed to feel the security of being married and having someone in the world to count on. Lloyd had been married briefly when he was twenty-five, only to have the marriage end badly, leaving him with a sense of failure that a successful marriage with me helped erase.

We married while I was still painting "Pasadena Livesavers." Lloyd was beginning a series of works that were to lead him to a personal, sculptural format that allowed him to speak of his own emotional states, though often even more indirectly than I. The link that existed in our work when I borrowed his symmetrical structure in 1963 had continued over the years, with mutual borrowing, influencing, and sharing of ideas. But even when we got married, we continued to live separately, feeling that it helped both of us maintain our separate identities. We had discovered that, although we had many things in common, our natural life styles were very different. I liked to get up in the morning and go directly about my business, going into my studio without talking to anyone. Then I liked to work all day and go out at night. Lloyd, on the other hand, preferred to work at night, sleep later than I, and he loved to talk in the morning. We also didn't like the same kinds of food: I preferred a broccoli and lamb chop diet (not exclusively, of course), while Lloyd liked one-dish dinners with very little meat. In 1971, when we finally began to live together again, we worked out a system of cooking our respective meals side by side and then eating together. But by that time we had both learned how to live according to our own needs and to help each other have the psychic privacy so essential to our work.

By the end of 1969, I felt that I was in a new place in my life and work. Painting "Pasadena Lifesavers," resolving and stabilizing my relationship with Lloyd, expressing my real experiences as a woman in lectures all conjoined to make me feel that I had more permission to be myself. I had not shown my work in Los Angeles for some time, and I decided that it was important to try to establish my range as an artist. I felt that I was not seen in the art world in a way that was commensurate with my achievements, and I still hoped that I could change that. I had been creating coherent bodies of work for some time, had worked across various media, including painting, sculpture, and process art, was dealing with the subject matter of my own identity as a woman, and had developed technical procedures in spraying and in fireworks that no one had done before. I wanted to share what I had done with my community, and arranged to have a show of the domes, the atmospheres in photo and film form, and the entire "Pasadena Lifesavers" series. I also wanted my being a woman to be visible in the work and had thus decided to change my name from Judy Gerowitz to Judy Chicago as an act of identifying myself as an independent woman.

The show, held at California State College at Fullerton, directed by Dextra Frankel, was beautiful, and Dextra's installation was fantastic. My name change was on the wall directly across from the entrance. It said:

Judy Gerowitz hereby divests herself of all names imposed upon her through male social dominance and freely chooses her own name *Judy Chicago*.

But, even though my position was so visibly stated, male reviewers refused to accept that my work was intimately connected to my femaleness. Rather, they denied that my statement had anything at all to do with my art. Many people interpreted the work in the same way they interpreted my earlier, more neutralized work, as if I were working only with formal issues. Admittedly the content of the work was not clear, but it seems that people could have made an effort to see the work in relation to the statement I had chosen to include. Moreover, no one even dealt with the range of ideas expressed or with the discrepancy between my status as an artist in the world and the obvious level of my development. Instead, there was only denial. At that time, there was no acknowledgment in the art community that a woman might have a different point of view than a man, or if difference was acknowledged, that difference meant inferiority.

As I look back on this, I realize that many issues were involved in the situation. I had come out of a formalist background and had learned how to neutralize my subject matter. In order to be considered a "serious" artist, I had *had* to suppress my femaleness. In fact, making a place as an artist had depended upon my ability to move away from the direct expression of my womanliness. Although I was trying to make my images clearer, I was still working in a frame of reference that people had learned to perceive in a particular, non-content-oriented way. But what other frame of reference existed then for abstract art? I was expecting the art community to actually "see" my work differently, to look at it in new terms, to respond to it on an emotional level. I realize that most people didn't know how to "read form" as I did. When Miriam Schapiro, the well-known painter from the East Coast who had recently moved to L.A., brought her class to the show, it was obvious that she could "read" my work, identify with it, and affirm it. On the other hand, a male artist friend of mine had told me: "Judy, I could look at these paintings for twenty years and it would never occur to me that they were cunts." The idea that my forms were cunts was an oversimplification, obviously, but at that time, even a greatly simplified perception seemed better than no perception at all of the relationship between my femaleness and my art.

When the achievement and meaning of my show went unrecognized, I was very upset. Not only had the exhibition not resulted in an increased understanding of my stature and intent as an artist, but it had produced a level of denial of my integrity that appalled me. I was accused of "mixing up" politics and art, "taking advantage" of the women's movement, of being "rigid" because I used a structure in my paintings, and of copying a male artist in my domes. I wanted my show to speak to people, to tell them that women possessed all aspects of human personality, that society's conception of the female was distorted and that other values in the culture that grew out of that distortion were also questionable. Fundamental to my work was an attempt to challenge the values of the society, but either my work was not speaking, society didn't know how to hear it, or both.

The full impact of my alienation struck me. I had tried to challenge society's conception of what it is to be a woman. At the same time, I had, in trying to make myself into an artist who was taken seriously in a male-dominated art community, submerged the very aspects of myself that could make my work intelligible. How could I make my voice heard, have access to the channels of the society that allow one's work to be visible, and be myself as a woman? I had tried to deal with the issues that were crucial to me "within" the structure of male art language and a male-oriented art community, a group whose values reflected the patriarchal culture in which we live. My accommodation had been self-defeating, however, for I could see by the results of my show and the evidence of my life as an artist that the male-dominated value structure, by its very nature, could not give me what I wanted and deserved. To honor a woman *in her own terms* would require a fundamental change in the culture and in the cultural values as they are expressed in art.

Men had constructed their community on the basis of their interests and needs as men. I realized that men (and women invested in that male community) *could not* respond to my work the way I wanted them to. There was no frame of reference in 1970 to understand a woman's struggle, to value it, or to read and respond to imagery that grew out of it. What did men know or care about what a struggle it was for a woman to overcome her conditioning as a woman, to feel comfortable about being assertive, to struggle to use tools that she had never been educated to use? And even if the male world could acknowledge that struggle, could it ever allow it to be considered "important" art, as important as the art that grew out of men's lives? I could not be content with having my work seen as trivial, limited, or "unimportant" if it dealt openly with my experiences as a woman, something I had seen happen to women who had not neutralized their subject matter. I also could no longer accept denying my experiences as a woman in order to be considered a "serious" artist, especially if my stature was going to be diminished anyway by the male-dominated community.

I realized that if the art community as it existed could not provide me with what I needed in order to realize myself, then I would have to commit myself to developing an alternative and that the meaning of the women's movement was that there was, probably for the first time in history, a chance to do just that. If my needs, values, and interests differed from male artists' who were invested in the values of the culture, then it was up to me to help develop a community that was relevant to me and other women artists. In fact, I was beginning to suspect that the reason there were so few visible women artists signified that the art community, as it existed, could not really serve the needs of women artists, unless they were willing to do what I had done and make art that did not deal directly with their experiences as women.

Perhaps I and other women would have to develop all aspects of an art community ourselves—making art, showing art, selling and distributing it, teaching other women artmaking skills, writing about art, and establishing our own art history, one that allowed us to discover the contributions of women artists past and present. I had been reading women's novels for several years, having given up male literature because I couldn't respond to the female characters. I had found a wealth of work by women I never knew existed, work with which I identified, and I was sure that there must likewise be unknown visual art by women. If making art according to male standards had resulted in making my subject matter unintelligible, perhaps looking at the work of women artists would give me clues about how to communicate my point of view more directly. But first, I would have to go back to the point where I had begun to hide my content and learn how to expose rather than cover that content.

I didn't know how to do that in Los Angeles, where the values of the male art community pervaded the environment —values that asserted form over content, protection over exposure, toughness over vulnerability. I decided to go away from the city for a year, to look for a job at a college, something that I had never done before, having supported myself by teaching occasional extension classes. When I graduated from college I had vowed not to become involved with day school teaching, as I didn't want to be like my teachers who had become more invested with their teaching than their art-making. Now I wanted to teach—but I wanted to teach women. I wanted to try to communicate to female students, to tell them what I had gone through in making myself into an artist. I felt that by externalizing the process I had gone through, I could examine it, which would be the first step in turning it around, and the women's class might also be the first step in making an alternative female art community.

I didn't know for sure if my struggle was relevant to other women, and I needed to find that out before I could use it as the basis for such a community. I felt a strong need to be with other women (something I had never done) and to find out if my own needs as an artist, my desire to build a new context, and the needs of other women interested in art could merge to become the basis for a viable female art community. I also felt a need to be in a place where male values were not as pervasive, and that meant a place where the art scene had less power. I wanted to feel safer, to open myself, to try to reverse the toughening process I had undergone in order to have a place in the male world. Also, I felt that if I worked with female students and helped them work directly out of their feelings as women, I could, through them, go back to that moment in my development where I began to move away from my own subject matter. I had decided to make another series of paintings. After having dealt with issues about the nature of my own identity as a woman, I wanted to move out, to go beyond my female identity into an identity that embraced my humanness. I wanted to make paintings that were vulnerable, delicate, feminine, but that also reflected the skills I had developed in the male-dominated world. I needed the support of a female environment to expose myself more than I had been able to at that point, and I hoped, by establishing a class for women, that I could provide a context for my students and for me that could serve us all.

At that time in California, schools around the state were hiring Los Angeles artists who "had a reputation," and although my reputation was not consistent with my development, I had made somewhat of a name for myself as an artist. Because of that, I found it fairly easy to get a job. I simply put out the word that I was looking and sent a few notes to places that, I had been informed, were hiring. I received a telephone call from Fresno State College, which I had never heard of. They were very eager to have me come there— so eager, in fact, that they were willing to accommodate me in any way, especially after they received a recommendation from my former sculpture teacher that "the best way to work with me was to let me do what I wanted."

Lloyd and I discussed it. We went up there to look around, and as soon as we drove into the city, I knew that it was the perfect place for me to be for a year. In addition to the other reasons that I wanted to go away, I felt that I should learn to live without Lloyd "being up the street from me," as his presence sometimes provided me with a way of avoiding acting independently. The year apart was difficult for us. Lloyd resented it and was forced by my absence to struggle with his feelings that I should "be there" whenever he needed me, an illusion he had even when we weren't getting along. My leaving the city accentuated my insistence that Lloyd not look to me as his only source of emotional support. At the same time, I put myself into a position where I would be forced to provide for myself in a way I had not yet learned to do. The Fresno year allowed me to examine my ambitions and make plans for my life in terms of my own needs, goals, and desires. It gave me the space that I needed to think, to dream, to experiment, and to change.

Fresno and the
Women's Program

Before I was hired at Fresno State, I discussed my ideas for a female art class with the Art Department chairman, a man who considered himself a "liberal." He was very sympathetic toward my plan to offer a class for women only, and we discussed the fact that a great many young women entered the beginning art classes and few emerged from the schools into professional life. He agreed with me that something should be done about that, and he seemed to understand my desire to give back some of my own acquired knowledge to younger women. I did not discuss my experiences in the male art community, nor did I mention my plan to develop an alternative context for women. I stressed my interest in helping young women become artists and, because Fresno was outside of the sophisticated art world, there was little real comprehension of the implications of my plan.

I posted signs in the halls of the Art Department, inviting

young women who wanted to be artists to come to a meeting where I discussed my ideas about a class. On the posters and in my remarks, I stressed that the women should want to be artists because I felt that my struggle, if it was relevant to other women, was so primarily to those who had already developed to the point that they had a desire to "do" something with their lives. However, one of the first things that I discovered in working with the class was that asking the women if they wanted to be artists was not a reliable question because many of them did not have the assurance that they could actually become what they said they wanted to become. Once I knew that I *wanted* to be an artist, I had made myself into one. I did not understand that wanting doesn't always lead to action. Many of the women had been raised without the sense that they could mold and shape their own lives, and so, wanting to be an artist but without the ability to realize their wants was, for some of them, only an idle fantasy, like wanting to go to the moon.

I had made a tentative plan for the class. I suspected, from my own struggle, that the reason women had trouble realizing themselves as artists was related to their conditioning as women. I had found that society's definition of me as a woman was in conflict with my own sense of personhood (and, after all, it was a *person* who was making art). Due to my own determination, I had been able to stand up to this conflict and to function in the face of it. If my situation was similar to other women's, then my struggle was a metaphor for the struggle out of role conditioning that a woman would have to make if she were to realize herself. I was sure that this process would take some time, and so I set up the class with the idea that I would work intensely with the fifteen women I had chosen for a year. When I began to realize how primitive their self-images were, I began to doubt whether a year would be long enough, as it seemed that before I could even help them make art, I would have to help them feel that they were "all right" as people.

I had decided that the class should meet away from the campus because I had had ample demonstrations of how intimidated many young women are in the presence of men. When I had lectured in the Los Angeles area, speaking about my ideas for a female art community and expressing the facts of my personal struggle, I had held question-and-answer periods afterward. Frequently, only men would raise their hands. Feeling that it was ludicrous to discuss these issues only with men, I had asked the men to leave. Only after they had gone did the women begin to assert themselves, soon becoming lively and uninhibited. The change that so often takes place in women when men are present was further illustrated to me after my all-female class started in Fresno. During the first semester, I also taught a mixed class, and several of the women from the all-female class were in that. On Monday, in the segregated class, the women were assertive, eager, and outspoken. On Tuesday, in the mixed class, the same women became passive and withdrawn. It is not that the men did anything overt to cause the women to retreat; rather, their presence reminded the women of society's tacit and all-pervasive instruction that they should not be too aggressive, so that the men's egos would not be threatened. This ever-present command seemed to be lifted only when men were not around, for me then as well as them.

In order to have a space in which we could explore ourselves without the intimidating presence of men, I felt that we should have a studio away from the school. Besides, being an artist meant having a studio, and if I wanted the women to experience themselves as artists, I thought the first step would be for them to do what artists do—find a studio, fix it up, then begin to work in it. The fixing-up process seemed a natural way for the women to learn to use tools, develop building skills, and gain confidence in themselves physically. I remembered my own phony bravado in the industrial arts shop and felt committed to providing a way for the women to learn craft without either having to "come on tough" or feel embarrassed about their awkwardness. I also thought that, once the studio was complete, we would get an old car and fix it up, thus further extending mechanical skills and also helping the women build a sense of independence. I wanted them to feel that they could "take care of themselves"—something, it turned out, few of them felt.

Only after these processes had taken place did I plan to move into artmaking, but my plans changed and adapted themselves to the natural flow of the group. The first meeting of the class freaked me out. The fifteen students and I were sitting around at the home of one of the women. The women were chitchatting, talking about clothes and boyfriends in a very superficial manner. I sat quietly for a while, waiting for them to start talking about their feelings about the class, their excitement or fear, their ideas about art, a book one of them had read, anything that would indicate some intellectual interest. But the conversation never altered from its course— clothes, boyfriends, casual experiences, food. I couldn't believe it. I had been with art students before. There was generally *some* discussion about something having to do with art or the arts in general. I suddenly felt panicked. What had I gotten myself into? This was just like high school. I had run away from this . . . I didn't want to be identified with women like these . . . "chicks," who concerned themselves with trivial issues. I didn't know what to do . . . I wanted to escape. I forced myself to stay, to take responsibility for my feelings. Right then, I made the most important step in my commitment to women: to always reveal exactly how I felt. I said: "You know, you are boring the hell out of me. You're supposed to be art students. Art students talk about art and books and movies and ideas. You're not talking about anything."

Dead silence. I thought: "Already the first day and I, with my big mouth, have blown it." Then I heard a soft voice saying: "Well, maybe the reason we don't talk about anything is that nobody ever asked us what we thought." I was very moved. I realized that no one had ever demanded of these women that they reach their potential. They began to tell me about their lives and relationships, about how, when they went to parties, the men did most of the "serious talking." True, many of them had been pressured by their parents into getting good grades, but getting good grades was one thing, and establishing personal goals and identities was another. They were always introduced as Sue or Carol or Nancy, just "girls" who were expected to go along with the men. (Later, we developed a practice of always introducing ourselves and each other by our full names and shaking hands, looking full into the face of the person to whom we were being introduced.) We discussed the idea of making demands upon each other, about learning to exchange ideas, feelings, and thoughts. Soon the room was filled with discussion and excitement. It would not be until the following year that I would begin to understand the full implications of making demands upon personalities who were accustomed to being protected, not pushed. But I had to be involved with female education for several years before its dynamic became clear.

During the first semester, the class met two days a week for four hours a day. There were several studio-hunting teams, but until we found a place, we met at the house of one of the women. I didn't know about classical consciousness-raising then. Instead we did a kind of modified consciousness-raising, which combined the expressing of common experiences with my trying to help the women understand the implications of those experiences in order to change their behavior patterns. It had become clear that one of the reasons that many of the women did not work consistently at their art (a common problem among female art students) was that their personal lives were very confused. One woman, for example, was living with a man who was totally dependent upon her. They had no sexual relationship. She took care of him; he gave her almost nothing in return. In a few weeks, the group, which was beginning to question the conditioned assumptions many of them had about their lives, asked her why she put up with that situation. She thought about it and realized it was in order to "have a boyfriend," no matter how empty the relationship really was. She saw that she did not *have to have* a man; she realized that she could make her own life meaningful *in itself,* an important step in building her identity as an artist.

In order to help the women establish stronger personal identities, I had to become involved with them and their lives. I had mixed feelings about doing that, but I understood that only if I found out about their particular personality structures would I be able to unravel the things that blocked them in developing themselves. It is important to point out that I had chosen to work with young college women, and the problems that I encountered related to the level of development they were at. All my suspicions about role conditioning and its

effect on young women's growth were confirmed in Fresno. I
had been able to overcome my conditioning because I had
been brought up to believe that I could do what I wanted.
Few of the women I have worked with in Fresno or thereafter
had that same confidence. The Fresno experience provided
me with information about the needs of relatively undeveloped
women. In the Extension Classes I had taught, I had always
encouraged my students to participate, feeling uncomfortable
about "laying a rap on them." At the first meeting of a class,
I would outline my plans for the class and then ask the students what they thought about what I said. Generally, there
would be little response. Most of the students probably
thought that I was asking that question more out of form
than because I really wanted an answer. I guess they figured
that, if they didn't say anything, that would be just as well,
because then I could launch into my "trip," something they
learned most college teachers did. But I was as uncomfortable
with the rigid student/teacher interaction as I was with the
standard male/female role. I wanted *real* interaction, and
knowing that the students would test me to see if they could
get me to play "teacher," I had developed a technique that
invariably worked. When there was no response, I told them
I was prepared to sit through the entire class time in silence
if they didn't want to participate, but I was not prepared to
talk *at* them. Generally, after ten to twenty minutes of silence,
the students couldn't stand it any more and would begin talking.

Once one of them began to talk, then I asked another
what he or she thought. Soon, the whole group would be
talking to each other. Each week, I would do the same
thing until there began to be a group spirit, which could sustain the class *whether I was there or not*. This technique

proved to be very valuable in working with women. Since many women feel too intimidated to speak, particularly at the beginning of a class, it often helps if they can sit in silence and struggle with themselves until they can say what they feel. And, of course, feeling that they won't be judged helps considerably. Additionally, developing a strong group takes much of the burden off the teacher, something I was grateful for as the year progressed. I am sure that being on the West Coast also contributed to the difficulty many of the women had in articulating their ideas and feelings. I have noticed that East Coast students seem more verbally agile, but I am sure that there are many places around the world where the women have the same problems that the Fresno women had.

Anyway, even before we had the term "consciousness-raising," I felt intuitively comfortable with its spirit, a spirit that could actually revolutionize teaching. I have often wondered about the "Who knows the answer, children?" method of education. Invariably, the children who have been reared in a verbally oriented home raise their hands, give the "right" answer and are dubbed "bright," while the silent children, who probably know the answer but don't feel confident in their ability to express it, are considered "dumb." These identities follow them through school. The wonderful thing about consciousness-raising is that, because one goes "around the circle," one discovers that the strangest people know the "right" answer.

As the class continued, all the students were becoming gradually more conscious of their situation as women in the culture. I felt that it was important for them to understand and be able to cope with their circumstances, instead of simply feeling, when they came up against cultural pressure, that there was "something wrong" with them. Their growing consciousness was a result, not only of our sessions, but also of their efforts to move out into the world. Looking for a studio had proved to be an educational process in itself. When they went to realtors' offices in search of commercial buildings instead of charming duplexes, the realtors refused to take them seriously and were incredulous when they informed them that there were looking for studio space for a group of women. Many male realtors refused to believe that women would want to "work" and insisted that they must want the place for parties. We spent a great deal of time discussing how to present oneself in the world so that one would be taken "seriously." We did some role-playing, the women alternately taking the parts of the realtors and themselves, acting out their experiences, trying to find new ways to respond to the realtors' doubts. Instead of feeling intimidated and just slinking out, they learned, through these methods, to challenge the men, demand the right to rent the place of their choice, and struggle to get what they wanted.

The class was as good for me as it was for the students. It was a wonderful experience to be able to share the struggles I had had and find that they were not only interesting and meaningful to the women, but provided them with information about how to help themselves. The one thing that I didn't understand at the time was that I had begun a process that was natural and organic. Once I had organized the class, taken it away from the school, given myself and the students a space of our own and a support group, provided them with a positive role model and an environment in which we could be ourselves, growth for all of us was inevitable. It almost didn't matter what we did as long as we were working at something productive. This suggests that what I stumbled on in Fresno has implications for all areas of female education.

Our meetings were very intense. We talked a lot about sex and parents and being independent. It has always been my contention that sexual behavior is a mirror of the total behavior of a person, and I have never, for example, been able to understand how someone can say that he or she has a terrible relationship but "great" sex. If one cannot act on one's needs in the world, articulate one's real feelings to another person, and feel good about one's wants, how can one do those same things in bed? These are things that seem fundamental to having a good sexual experience. At any rate, discussing sex illuminated the entire personality problems of the women in the class and also opened up an area for work sooner than I had thought possible. Since the real concerns of the women's lives revolved around their sexual anxieties, their problems with their boyfriends and parents, possible pregnancies, the impossibility of getting enough money for food working at the degrading and low-paying jobs available to them, I decided to see what would happen if I encouraged them to make art out of the things with which they were really involved. When they went to their other art classes, they were supposed to concern themselves with "form and shape and color and line" and other formal issues that had little to do with their actual day-to-day experiences.

In one of our sessions, we discussed how we felt when we walked down the street and were harassed by men. Everyone had very strong attitudes about these experiences, and we decided to try to make images of the feelings. I asked the women to deal with the sensation or experience of being psychically invaded by a man or men. There was no media restriction. They were free to paint, draw, write, make a film, or do a performance. On the day the work was presented, we were downstairs in the basement of one of the students' homes.

Everyone was trembling because women were showing images of feelings and experiences that none of us had ever seen portrayed before; paintings and drawings, poems, performances, and ideas for films, all revealing the way women saw men. These perceptions were considerably different from the way men saw and depicted themselves in their art.

One woman presented a performance that had to do with being asleep next to her boyfriend, dreaming that a man had come into the room and was stroking her leg slowly, panting with lust and excitement. She awoke, frightened, but as soon as she sat up, he disappeared. Was he real or was he an ever-present specter, whose need encroached upon her even while she was asleep? Again, she dozed, saw him, and woke up screaming. Again he disappeared. She became more and more confused and felt that there was no safety, no escape from male presence, which surrounded her, consumed her, invaded her, even in sleep.

The images that day came out with an incredible force, as if they had been bottled up and suddenly released. They were so powerful that they frightened me, but I didn't want the students to see my fears and become anxious about exposing what was clearly the raw material for an openly female-oriented art, as I felt that they were dependent upon me for support and strength. I had my own anxieties about exposure to deal with. I felt overwhelmed by the level of responsibility that had somehow implicitly come to rest with me, just by the fact of this class and the permission the women in it felt. I couldn't "pass the buck." I was the person responsible for providing that permission, and that was a terrifying feeling. Since it is essentially men who run the world, women rarely have the experience of feeling that if they don't take care of something, no one else will, except in the home. Not that I want to depreciate the level of responsibility for private and personal realities that women *have* to accept, just by being women. It is, however, unusual for that same level of responsibility to extend to women in the world. Now, I was faced with what seemed like enormous responsibility. These women needed my strength in order to grow. It frightened me.

I felt that I needed someone to turn to, someone who could give me the support I needed for trying to grow, to become independent, to not only take responsibility for my condition as a woman but to contribute to changing that condition. The only one I could think of who might be able to help me was Miriam Schapiro. She was teaching at a new art school called the California Institute of the Arts, in the north end of Los Angeles. I felt that because she herself was a realized painter and a strong woman, she would understand the struggle I was going through in trying to help these young women realize their own strengths. I had been very excited when I heard she had moved to the West Coast a few years before. She had been painting and exhibiting for a number of years in the East and I related to her work, which was primarily abstract. After she visited my show in Fullerton, I felt that she understood my work too. She had made her way in the art world during the heyday of Abstract Expressionism, which was a hotbed of *macho* attitudes. She had managed, in the face of many obstacles, to make a place for herself as an artist, and I admired her both personally and artistically. We had had a few conversations, and one time she had invited me to speak at the college in San Diego where she had previously been teaching. I knew that she supported my ideas about a women's class. Since she was older than I, I hoped that she would be able to provide me with the kind of support with which I was providing the students, who were younger than I.

I didn't know her that well, but I called her anyway. As soon as she answered the phone, I blurted out: "Miriam, this is Judy. Look, I have to talk to you." I hardly gave her a chance to answer when I continued: "All these things are happening up here in my women's class and they're frightening me." I told her about the images and about the power with which they were coming out. I explained that I was trying to provide an environment in which the women could work directly out of their feelings and experiences as women, something I had never had the chance to do, and I guessed, neither had she. She seemed to understand everything I said and was very reassuring, supportive, and helpful.

As I look back on that phone call, I realize that I was trying to run away from the level of responsibility I had unknowingly forced upon myself by establishing that class. I had discovered that the women I was working with were very damaged by their upbringing in male culture, more damaged than I had ever been. It was a shock to me to recognize that I had somehow come through the society without being wiped out and that many other women hadn't. The enormity of the situation overwhelmed me. I didn't want to face it alone. I didn't know how to. I had barely come out of my own struggle, and here I was starting another one. But what choice had I? If I didn't build another environment, then I was condemned to functioning exclusively within the male-dominated art community that allowed me only limited roles and recognition. If I didn't take responsibility for my situation as a woman, commit myself to other women, and make a new context, what could I do? I felt trapped.

I turned to Mimi for help, and in one way that was good. She helped me considerably during the two years we worked together. I needed an older woman, a mother figure, I guess, who could support *my* desire to be independent in the same way I was providing that kind of support for my students. I also needed a female peer, something I had never had. In some ways, Mimi was marvelous, but I needed her help so much that I was not really in a position to evaluate the interchanges that took place between us when she came up to Fresno or in the succeeding months of our relationship. I am not sure that, at that point, I was really in control of the process I had begun with her. Instead, I basked in the warmth of the help that she extended and allowed myself to believe that this "mother" would take care of me and help me build the new context that I so ardently desired.

Mimi came up to Fresno after we had moved into our studio. We had finally found an old place called the Community Theatre, and the women had painted it and fixed it up. I had helped them build a forty-foot-long dividing wall out of two-by-fours and sheetrock. For the women, that wall symbolized that they could accomplish anything they set out to do. For me, that wall taught me how deep a need I had to work with other women, to see my struggles reflected in theirs. I remember standing in the studio, watching the women hammer and nail and wrestle with those wooden beams. I felt that I could have stood there for five years and still never have enough of seeing women "work" together like that.

I had arranged for Miriam to give a lecture at the college. As it turned out, it was the first time she had ever been invited to talk about her work. Afterward, the women and I had a party for her. She came to our five thousand-square-foot studio, which had an office and a rap room whose floors were covered with rugs made by the women out of carpet scraps. There were big pillows all around. We had a kitchen and a large center studio space plus back rooms for painting and drawing. The women presented several performance pieces for Miriam, showed her their work, and shared their feelings with her. Miriam gave them wonderful feedback on their work, something they really needed. I was better at helping women get started than I was at providing criticism, but Mimi had a great gift for analyzing work. The women really responded to her and she to them. Not too long after that, Miriam and I began to discuss the possibility of working together and of bringing the class structure that I had started to Los Angeles, where we would teach together. Her husband was the dean of the Art School at the California Institute of the Arts, and she felt sure that he would be supportive of a women's program. Also, Lloyd was already teaching there and there was great interest at the school in husband-and-wife teams.

After the studio was finished, I decided that it was time to transfer the dependency of the group upon me to dependency upon the structure of the group itself. That way the group could provide support for each woman, rather than all the women looking to me, which again froze me into the "teacher" role. We had been asked to do a seminar at the University of California, Berkeley. The women did some of the performance pieces that they had shown Miriam. They presented themselves very well, so well that I felt they were ready for another step in growth. After the seminar, I told them that I wasn't going to relate to them any more primarily on an emotional level. Up until that time, we had been spending more energy dealing with personal problems than making art. I suggested that they begin to rely on each other for emotional raps, setting them up either regularly or on the basis of individual needs. I told them that henceforward I was going to relate to them almost entirely on the basis of work.

My strategy for the year had been to first help the women open up, then encourage them to turn to each other for support, and finally, to begin to demand that they relate to me as younger artists to an older artist—through work. This was very important because women do not ordinarily relate to each other on the basis of work. The women had become quite skilled at discussing their problems in depth and exposing their real feelings, but they were not nearly as good at translating those feelings into work, working regularly, setting work goals for themselves, and helping each other as much in their art problems as in their life problems.

Although all the women agreed that it was a good idea to begin to concentrate on work, there was a great deal of insecurity manifested in the group at this time. Crying jags, depressions, and self-deprecating remarks were rampant. The women weren't at all confident that they could make the change. Many of them were extremely angry at me for making demands upon them that they were afraid they couldn't meet. This lasted for about a month, during which time I tried to ignore most of their expressions of anxiety. Gradually they began to feel more sure of themselves. By the end of the first semester, the women were beginning to take control of the class. They set up work demands for themselves and each other. All of them wanted more time to work at their art and to be in the studio. I arranged with the college that they could have flexible credit, from six to fifteen units, depending upon how much work they did. The women set up the following system: six units of credit required four hours of daily work in the studio; nine units required six hours' daily work; and if you asked for twelve to fifteen units, you had to work at the studio eight hours a day. The schedule for the second semester was arranged almost completely by the women themselves. On Wednesday evenings, we had dinner meetings, to which everyone came. During the week, the women came and went as they pleased and had individual conferences with me as they needed them. There was a reading group in which we read books by women and examined them from the point of view: Did women in the past provide us with information about their lives that is either interesting or meaningful to us? I knew from my own reading that it was important to know that women before us had made good work and to be able to identify with that work.

If there was as much unknown women's art as there was women's literature, then surely all of us would benefit from knowing about it. I felt that it was important for the women to learn about the work of women of the past, identify with their lives, and use their achievements to extend their own. I personally wanted to see the work and examine it for clues that could help me in my own art. We organized a research seminar, and the women began to go to local libraries, then to libraries in Los Angeles, where they went through books, making lists of all the names of the women artists that they found. We quickly discovered that there was an enormous amount of information about women artists that had never been collated—so much, in fact, that I cried because I felt deprived of my rightful heritage. We resolved to put together the bits and pieces that we found and to make an archive at Cal Arts. Mimi used to have her assistant check out the books that the women had found in the library, take them to Cal Arts, make slides from them, then return them. Out of her pocket and mine and with the work of young students, we put together the first West Coast file on women artists' work.

By halfway through the year, it was very clear that our

"class" was tranforming itself into a community, a community based on *the students'* needs as well as mine. The women really went through enormous struggles that year. The main emphasis of the "program," which is what we had begun to call it by then, was to plug into our own psyches and work with the material of our experiences in whatever way that material dictated. One of the most important discoveries of the year was that informal performance provided the women with a way of reaching subject matter for artmaking. The most powerful work of the first year of the program was the performances.

This fact led me to the conclusion that one of the reasons that so few women succeed in art schools is that the techniques for establishing a focus for the artmaking process arise primarily out of the cultural education of men. Thus, in sculpture classes, male students "get going" by doing simple problems with materials, techniques, etc. At a faculty meeting, while I was at Cal Arts, a male sculpture teacher was discussing his projects for beginning students. He intended to give them a long four-inch-by-four-inch piece of wood and ask them to cut it on the saw, making sections they could then join together. The project was conceived in terms of what men were expected to do and to know—that is, how to use saws, what a four-by-four was, and what you could do with it. Most female students, if they were like the students that I have worked with, probably couldn't relate to that project as being meaningful. This teacher probably never thought about the fact that his female students would bring a different background to his class than would his male students, and would probably get the message from his projects that sculpture was just not for them.

In fact, it has always amazed me that no thought has

ever been given in colleges and universities around the country that until one hundred years ago, women were not allowed access to institutions of higher learning. When they were finally accepted into colleges, they were treated as if they were just like men, as if they had not just stepped out of a centuries-long cultural tradition and education quite unlike men's. No one seems to have asked: Do women have different needs than men because they have been housekeeping, raising children, quilting, sewing, cooking, weaving, nurturing, pleasing men, and remaining in the background, while men ran the world? Also, since most women are raised to value feeling over abstract ideas, responsiveness over assertiveness, and small scale over large, does it not seem ludicrous to ask them to move out of their frame of reference and into another without as much as a gulp?

The class continued. Each of the women paid twenty-five dollars per month toward rent, equipment, and materials. At the beginning of the year, we had had a lengthy discussion about buying tools, which I had urged the women to do. Many of them objected, saying that if they wanted a hammer, they'd go borrow one; if they needed some wood, they'd find a house that was being torn down. I tried to explain to them that if you had a hammer at your disposal it suggested the building of something. If you had a tape recorder, it suggested recording something. If you had a movie camera, it suggested making a film. They were unconvinced, but they went along with the plan. By the second half of the year, they were all making frequent use of those tools, cameras, and equipment, and had come to realize the necessity of having things easily obtainable. One of the women built a darkroom and was teaching other women how to take, develop, and print their own pictures, while others were crewing for each other's films, helping each other with their projects and exchanging skills with each other.

I was making plans, with Miriam, to bring the program to Cal Arts. A number of the women had decided that they wanted to go with me. Miriam helped them prepare their portfolios, and eight of the original women were accepted into the school. The year was almost over. We had a weekend rap session and invited women from Fresno, Los Angeles, and San Francisco to the studio. We put up drawings, paintings, and photographs. Many of the drawings were filled with vaginas, uteruses, ovaries, and breasts, as my early work had been, not because I had urged women to use that imagery, but because it had come out naturally. But there was no one to make the women feel uncomfortable about revealing their femininity. The women performed their pieces and showed their films. There were three plays. One was called the *Rivalry Play* and dealt with two women who met at a bus stop. One of them was elegant, well-dressed, proud. The other was fat, sloppy, ill-mannered, and poorly dressed. While waiting for the bus, they began to irritate each other. Their initial dislike quickly escalated to competition and rivalry until finally they began to fight, each trying to overcome the other in an age-old feud between women who fight each other because they cannot fight their real oppressor. Their fight resulted in murder, each killing the other, in whose eyes they saw themselves and their own self-hatred.

Another piece involved two women, one dressed as a man, perhaps a butcher. "He" led the woman out onto the stage, tying her to a milking machine. Then, giving her a nudge, "he" walked out, leaving her to squirt blood from the machine into a pitcher until it was full. All the time, a tape recorder played, telling of the proceedings at a slaughterhouse.

After the woman was finished, the man returned. He tied her up by her hands and then, as slides of meat and parts of mutilated cattle were shown, he poured the blood/milk she had "given" onto her body. The last slide was cattle strung up by their haunches, projected onto the bloody body of the woman, an image of woman's brutalization, another common theme used by the students that year.

Several films were shown that weekend. One was about a woman going to the market, getting a steak, cooking it, and eating it. It was an unremarkable subject, except that it showed women in a new way. In the *Steak Film,* as in another, collaborative film, the *Bathtub Film,* women were shown eating, bathing, and enjoying themselves alone, not in relation to a man. All of the work done by the women dealt with or revealed some aspect of their experiences as women. Theirs was content-oriented art. Although I never instructed them to make any particular kind of work, I had encouraged them to use the content of their lives as the basis of their art and that had stimulated the production of a lot of work. The women in the audience were generally very excited by what they saw and the weekend was filled with identification, laughter, tears, and warmth. I cried, feeling that the weekend had somehow changed the meaning of the year. Now what we were doing was out in the open. Other people were seeing it and sharing it. It was like being at the moment of birth, the birth of a new kind of community of women, a new kind of art made by women.

Many of the women managed, in one year, to change their lives, alter their personality structures, develop leadership, make art, write about their experiences, speak and perform publicly, learn building and filmmaking skills. They did costuming, makeup, and sewing one day, construction work the

next, and art-history research in the evening, moving easily
from one discipline to another, regardless of their previous
experience in that discipline. Several of the women came
into the program entirely on the basis of their own determination that they wanted to be part of it. Some of them had no
art skills at all; others had been discouraged by male teachers
from continuing with their work. And yet they succeeded because they were in an environment that allowed them to be
themselves and that demanded excellence from them.

The experiences of the Fresno women imply that our notions about who can or cannot be artists need re-evaluation
and that our educational systems are allowing the potential of
women to remain untapped. I have, since that year, traveled
around the country, lecturing and working with women.
Again and again I have discovered that the women in the
various art programs are being virtually untouched by their
education. They sit in classes taught primarily by men, look
at slides of work done almost exclusively by male artists, and
are asked to work on projects that have little to do with their
lives and concerns. If they make images that are relevant to
the facts of their femaleness, they are put down, ignored,
laughed at, or rejected. Is it any wonder that few young
women succeed in becoming serious artists? Often women
pay large amounts of money for an entirely inadequate education. Why? Primarily because they do not understand that
there can be alternatives. Additionally, not enough women of
achievement have yet accepted the responsibility to provide
for younger women by committing themselves to the education of women. In many ways, I understand the reluctance
some women feel to take on this task. It requires that one
really face one's situation as a woman in a male-dominated
culture, and that is extremely difficult. It involves recogniz-

ing that one does not always have the "privilege" of just doing one's work. It demands a high level of social responsibility, often seen as inconsistent with the role of the artist. But I felt at the time that I had no choice.

If a woman recognizes, as I did, that the only way women can ever live in real dignity is to make the society a place where both men and women can share its responsibilities and rewards equally, then she must commit herself to the struggle for women's freedom. Coming to grips with this has been very difficult for me. Even now, I feel resentful that my choice is to submit or to fight. I have to live in a narrow stratum of reality, because I cannot bear the values that are reflected in the movies, on TV, in popular magazines, even in the art museums. I tried to close my eyes to the fact that society's contempt for women is really a reflection of a distortion in the entire value system that emphasizes competition, exploitation, and the objectification of human beings, both men as well as women. But once I faced it I had to take responsibility to try to change it. The year in Fresno was the first step.

5

Returning to Los Angeles

During the year in Fresno, I made two series of large paintings, one called "Fresno Fans," the other entitled "Flesh Gardens." The "Fresno Fans" were five feet by ten feet and
were structured on a system of boxes, each sprayed so that
they fanned in or out. This made the sections breathe, open
and close, expand and contract. The centers were bars, slits,
or squares. The structure of the painting was based upon a
body gesture that reached out from that center and extended
to the corners of the paintings. The "Flesh Gardens" were
eight feet by eight feet. They were also based on a series of
squares and, although the structure of the paintings was rigid,
the color was soft and open. The format was strong and assertive, the image was fleshy and vulnerable. Both series were
related to my desire to "reach out" from my female identity
into something larger. Thus, while the centers of the paintings
referred to my femaleness, the image also implied land-
scape: sky, sun, grass.

The studies for the paintings included written notations:

"How can I make a hard shape soft?" I asked. "How can I fit a soft shape into a hard framework?" I had been educated in the tradition of male art, and while some of that education was important to me, much of it was still restrictive. My consciousness as a woman had developed still farther in Fresno, yet my art didn't seem to reveal that clearly. I felt trapped by the structure that I used in my paintings. On the one hand, that structure allowed me to establish a format against which my intuition could play. Perhaps the paintings grew out of that part of myself that was still struggling to put together my own impulses with the art background that I knew. I had been preparing to paint those paintings for a long time —first developing the technical skills that would allow me to work so large, then establishing color systems that could speak of hard and soft, open and closed, strong and receptive.

The Fresno paintings revealed the dilemma I was in. "How to fit a soft shape into a hard framework?" How can I, a woman, fit my impulses into an aesthetic format that is rigid, hard, impersonal? Those paintings were about a confrontation between two sets of values. And still the content was hidden. When I started to make the first "Fan" painting, I had to paint it three times. Each time, I started out making the center very soft, very open, very exposed. Each time, I became frightened and covered it up again, "coming on strong" as I had learned to do in the male art community, learned to do in order to protect that soft center, to keep it from being destroyed. Now I wanted to open it up and I couldn't.

As the months passed and I helped my students open themselves, I absorbed some of the permission I was giving them. There was no one to give me what I needed, and so I gave to myself by giving to my students. They were building their art directly out of their experiences as women. I could hardly even reveal my subject matter openly, much less find a way to make it speak clearly. Yet I had artmaking skills, and they didn't. They had permission to be themselves and no skills to convey their information. I had skills but no ability to make direct contact with my impulses. The gap that existed between me and my students seemed to be the same gap that exists between women in the professions and those outside of them. It is a gap that I was unknowingly committing myself to bridge as I struggled in my studio that year to make "serious" art that could also communicate my personal realities.

At one point in the year, I began to work in the women's studio. The group had developed coherence and a sense of community. I felt that I had helped them make that community, and still I felt alienated from it. My age alienated me. My experience alienated me. My professionalism alienated me. I was jealous of my students, jealous that they were having an opportunity to do something that I had not had. I had painted these large, technically formidable paintings and, although they were beautiful, they still did not speak the language of my real self.

By the end of the year, I felt that I would have to give up the painting methods I knew. I thought that I would have to be like my students, begin all over again and build my art out of the new permission that I was establishing for them. I decided that the next year, when I went back to Los Angeles, I would work more completely with the women of the program. I wanted to bring my art and my feminism together, and I did not see how to do it with the artmaking methods I had. I saw all these new possibilities opening up before me. I had formed my life at an earlier time in history, a time when there were fewer opportunities than there were now. I could see all these roads stretching out from my developing consciousness toward a new art, a new literature, a new theater, new kinds of collaboration among artists, perhaps even a new relationship between artist and society. I wanted to start all over again. For the first time in my life, I had no new ideas for art—only a desire to move out, beyond anything I had yet done. I couldn't fit my forms into a rigid structure. That was the answer. I would have to abandon the structure.

In July, I packed up my studio and made plans to return to Los Angeles. Lloyd and I had decided that we would try to live together again. He had found a strange rambling house for us, where we both had small studios. After a year apart, we both felt the need to be close and to try to weave our lives back together. Lloyd was teaching at Cal Arts. Now I was going there too, along with eight of my students and the concept of female education in art that had begun in Fresno. By that time, Mimi and I were very close. We spent a great deal of time together, discussing, planning, struggling. At one point in the year, we had presented a slide talk on women's art. Building from our own imagery, we analyzed a number of abstract paintings and sculptures. We found that many women seemed to have done what both of us had—hidden a personal content in an artmaking style that was close to that being done by the men around them. In many cases, the stylistic differences among the women's work were striking, but the content came through nonetheless. Our own artmaking experiences made us able to perceive it. We had presented the material to a group of women in New York. Some of them reacted with hostility, some recognized their own impulses in the work, and still others realized they were seeing the first step in a new kind of art history, one that searched out women's work for women's point of view.

The Fresno experiment had been an incredible success. We

had put out an issue of a Los Angeles feminist magazine, *Everywoman,* and it had circulated around the country. Suddenly I found myself visible in a way I had never been before. People wrote to me, asked me about what I was doing. I liked it and I was afraid simultaneously. I still felt anxious about the responsibility, but I felt that my relationship with Mimi would take some of that off my shoulders. It was exciting and it was scary, and when I came back to Los Angeles, I didn't know what would happen. In Fresno, there was not much of an art community, and the women's program had existed in a kind of a vacuum. The Los Angeles art community had sophisticated art standards. The cloistered isolation of Fresno wasn't appropriate there. Yet I didn't know how the male-oriented art community would receive me, my new ideas, or the Feminist Art Program, the official name of the women's program at Cal Arts.

Establishing an environment in which young women could be themselves and work out of their own experiences was only the first step toward the development of a female art community. Even if a new kind of work was made by women, it would still have to funnel back into an art system controlled by men. It was imperative to make another step in developing a female art community, one that would allow the work made by women to be seen in a context other than the male system. All over the country by that time, women artists were getting together, talking to each other. The same spirit that had inspired me was inspiring other women to come out of the isolation that had made us separate and self-despairing. There was a good deal of discussion beginning then about a female sensibility in art, partly stimulated by the slide show Mimi and I had put together, which by then we had shown on both coasts.

I decided that it would be a good idea to gather a group of women artists together, to rap about our needs and feelings about our art. It happened that Dextra Frankel was interested in doing a women's show. She, like me, had come to realize that she didn't know the work of very many working women artists. She asked me to help her put the show together, which offered me a perfect opportunity to go around to meet women artists on the West Coast, some of whom I knew, others whom I had never heard of. Frequently, Mimi went with us on our visits. Over the summer of 1971, we visited about fifty studios.

One thing we discovered on our visits was that we all had certain notions about what a studio was, based on our involvement with the male art community and our adaptation to it. We were accustomed to thinking of a studio as a loft or commercial space and were shocked that our visits took us to bedrooms, dining rooms, and porches more often than to two thousand square feet of commercial white space. I found it difficult, at first, to "see" the work, because it was not in the kind of space that I had learned designated importance and seriousness. Some women made studios right in the midst of their home environment and developed an artmaking process that was compatible with their life styles. Others worked in the back rooms of their men's studios, having internalized the idea that their work was less important. The bedroom studio or the back-room studio both marked the women artists with the stamp of dilettantism, even if their work was good, for if an artist's work is not surrounded by the kind of studio that men view as the mark of professionalism, it is not taken seriously. We had to overcome this cultural prejudice before we could fully appreciate the work.

As we traveled to more studios, we saw that some women

had an attitude toward artmaking that was strikingly different from men's. Many women had an interpenetration between their life and their art that made it hard to distinguish
where one left off and the other began. Objects, toiletries,
children's toys, pets, old postcards and curios, paintings, and
drawings all intermingled in a rich, womanly environment.
Although there are male artists who live in similar surround-
ings, they are usually considered eccentrics and unusual,
whereas this art/life style was common to a great number of
women, who fit their artmaking into a multiplicity of activities that included making breakfast, getting the children
off to school, doing the laundry, painting; then, while waiting
for the paint to dry, doing the dishes, after which it was back
into the studio until the children came home.

I saw two clear patterns in the lives of the women artists
that we visited. Some women worked in almost total isolation,
unknown to or ignored by the art community. Generally,
these artists worked with subject matter connected to their
home lives or their experiences as women. They tended to
work in the house and to be no part of the art world. Another
group of women artists, those whose work was more neutralized, as Mimi's and mine had been, were more connected to
the art world. They often had stores and lofts for studios, but
their relationship to the art world at that time was quite
peripheral, and many of them complained of blatant discrimination. In the years since then, it is these women artists
who have tended to become visible as a result of the feminist
movement. We heard many stories of struggling to be taken
seriously, of trying to be recognized by male peers. One painter
worked on the scraps of her husband's canvases, despite the
fact that she was every bit as good an artist as he. Dextra
really became angry when she saw that and tried to give the

woman a lot of support for demanding a better deal for herself. The alternatives represented by the women's situations
were dismal indeed, and they were alternatives that I had
struggled with. Either be oneself as a woman in one's work
and live outside the art community or be recognized as an
artist at the price of hiding your womanliness. Everywhere
I looked I saw the same dilemma, and it only confirmed my
belief that the only way out was to establish an alternative
context in which one did not have to choose between "being
a woman and being an artist," as my old friend the art critic
had so aptly put it many years before.

I saw that the women who had opted for their personal
subject matter had suffered the price of never seeing their
work enter the world. The women like me whose work had
become visible had sacrificed a part of their personalities to
do so. At the time, I felt that no one should do that. Over
the years, I have come to think that all people should have the
right to work out of whatever aspect of their personalities they
choose. Because I was insecure about my own needs, I tended
to project my needs on all women and say, "All women
should do such and such." As I became more relaxed about
my own identity and felt less afraid that I would be rejected
if I expressed my true self, I modified my "shoulds" to apply
only to myself. I do however still feel that many women
artists wish to ignore their situation as women, and I don't
really think that that ultimately provides a healthy environment for one's work.

The range of work that we chose for the show reflected
the two alternatives that seemed to describe women's situation. There was work that was highly formal, without much
overt female imagery. Other work was more explicit, dealing
with kitchens, costumes, curtains. There was a consistent kind

of softness and an antiheroic attitude in much of the work. The show revealed the still unrealized qualities of women's work, qualities that are sure to manifest themselves more openly as the new permission of the women's movement pervades the culture. It was interesting to note that few male artists appeared at the opening. Nonetheless, "Invisible/Visible," the title of the show, was one manifestation of the growing desire felt by women artists throughout the country to see each other's work, to search for self-reflection in the work of women, to show together, to stand together, and consequently to grow as women and as artists. It was the first time my work appeared in an all-female context, and I felt that it helped the content become more visible, as there was other work there that tried to bridge the gap between formalism and feminism. I also felt proud to be a part of the rapidly developing women artists' movement in America.

Lloyd was handling my involvement in the women's movement quite easily. If he felt threatened at all by it, it was probably because I seemed to have such a large group of friends by that time, all of whom offered support, encouragement, and comfort. Not only had my relationship with Mimi grown, but there were the Fresno women, all moved down and settled in the area. The year apart had helped Lloyd and me get our personal lives together to the point that we could move into a house and structure a life that allowed us both space. My relationships with people impinged on Lloyd somewhat, so I had to be careful to keep some of my activities out of the house.

We worked out a system in which we could both have the psychic privacy we needed to do our work. We established "silent days," where we would pass each other and not speak. This allowed us to be in the house together without feeling that we had to be accessible to the other person's needs all the time. We had learned how to communicate with each other very directly, saying: "I feel this or that, I need this or that." Rarely did we judge each other's needs by that time, feeling that after all, whether a need is "right" or "wrong," it is still a need. This allowed us to respond to each other openly and interact simply. Lloyd might say he needed to have some time alone. I would say "Sure," and then go about my business, figuring that I should make my own plans and that would be that. Once we reached the stage in our relationship that we had separated our personalities, then we found that we got along best if we were very straightforward with one another. By 1971, we had worked out a relationship in which, although we struggle, we both understand the nature of the struggle. This allows us to get through our infrequent arguments quickly and enjoy our relationship together.

However, although my marriage became smooth, the rest of my life continued to be a difficult road. I had committed myself to the establishment of an alternative art community. I had made the first step by setting up an educational program. I had connected with another woman artist and then with additional women artists, all of whom had expressed interest in establishing new structures for women. Throughout the fall of 1971, we met frequently. One weekend, we had a marathon, and all showed each other our work. At that session, Mimi initiated a discussion about a place to come together to share our work with the world. She inspired the other women to begin dreaming about such a place. Early in 1972, we held a Conference for Women Artists, the first in the country, at Cal Arts. Over two hundred women showed up, and it was just like our marathon. We all cried and laughed and shared our work and were overwhelmed at the number of artists there were and how good the work was.

Out of this conference came the plan for Womanspace, an exhibition space for women and a community art gallery, which opened in January 1973. By the time of the opening, those of us who had first planned an exhibition space, artists, some historians, critics, and collectors, had held many meetings with women around the art community. We did consciousness-raising at those meetings, explaining the origins of the plan—Dextra's show, the studio visits, the women artists' group, the conference. We must have met with hundreds of women, all of whom were somehow connected to art, either through the museums, art classes, private art activities, or just interest. But I am getting way ahead of myself. It is still 1971, and the Feminist Art Program opened at the California Institute of the Arts in Valencia.

The second year began quite differently from the first year in Fresno. We were to have studio space, private quarters, tools, equipment, course support money for projects and materials, an art historian, and a budget to continue our work in assembling female art history archives. This was to be the first time that a school of art was addressing itself specifically to the needs of its female students by incorporating an educational program designed and run by women. As it turned out, we didn't actually move into our official quarters until much later in the year. Mimi and I were interested in the possibility of starting with a large-scale art project. We wondered if it would be possible to deal with the problems women have making art *in* the context of work, rather than separate from it, as I had done in Fresno. Our art historian had suggested a project that we were quite enthused about, the designing of a house. Women had been embedded in houses for centuries and had quilted, sewed, baked, cooked, decorated, and nested their creative energies away. What would happen, we wondered, if women took those very same homemaking activities and carried them to fantasy proportions? Instead of making a pink-and-white, filmy, feminine but functional bedroom for one's daughter, the space might become pinker and whiter and filmier and filled with more and more ruffles until it was a complete environment. Could the same activities women had used in life be transformed into the means of making art?

The women in the program were as excited as Mimi and I about the house project. They broke up into teams and scoured the city for appropriate spaces. Three of the women spotted an old, run-down mansion near downtown Los Angeles, and finding the owner's name in the Hall of Records, wrote to her. She and her family agreed to let us use the house for three months. We estimated that it would take us two months to work on the space, and we wanted one month to exhibit the results.

On a bright November morning, twenty-three of us (twenty-one students, Mimi, and I) arrived at Mariposa Street armed with mops, brooms, saws, ladders, hammers, and nails. "Womanhouse" had begun. We looked around the seventeen rooms of the dilapidated old house and began to dream. Some women had visited the house already and made elaborate plans. Others were inspired by their first visit to choose a room they felt could be used for their fantasy environment. The first job was to get the house into shape for the transformation that was to be wrought. The house had been unoccupied for twenty years and had been repeatedly vandalized. The railing in the staircase had been ripped out, windows were broken, the toilets were stuffed up, dirt and grime were everywhere. The walls were peeling, the floors were covered with dusty carpets, and most of the cabinet doors were unhinged. We set to work: cleaning, scrubbing, tearing up carpets, repairing broken doors. Many women had plans for their rooms that required the building of walls, and furniture, plastering, wallpapering, and painting. They learned to use power tools so that they could build walls; learned how to run power sanders in order to trim the edges of furniture; discovered how to plaster as they repaired the broken walls of their rooms. Women taught women. Women helped each other saw and nail and build and carry things. When we needed to find out about replacing the twenty-five broken windows, the father of one of the women, who owned a hardware store, offered help. Several women went to his shop and came back with glass, putty, and know-how. We used fifty gallons of white paint on the walls, and by the end of the month, the house was beginning to shape up.

At first, it was difficult to get everyone working at a consistent pace. Several women, used to coming and going in classes, unobserved by male teachers, had a hard time learning that they were needed by the other women and that their absence was noticed. Some of the women thought that the eight-hour-day work load was outrageous, even though we had made it clear at the beginning of the year that that was one of the demands of the program. Those who had come from Fresno were accustomed to the work demand. But the other women were used to working when they felt like it, rather than on a daily schedule. But Mimi and I felt that regular working hours were important, because women do not usually have sufficient drive and ambition to keep them at a job when it becomes frustrating. This was certainly true of a number of our students, who had histories of uncompleted work. We thought that the women needed to learn about a continuity of work and about pushing past the frustration that results from a large-scale project. Few of the women had ever been involved in anything as overwhelming in scale and concept as the house was.

There was a lot of resentment about the demands that were being made: to be there every day; to do unaccustomed physical labor, which many of them were unaccustomed to; to push beyond their emotional and physical limits. They complained of being tired, of having aches and pains. Some women were extremely concerned about their bodies, in an overprotective way. They had been raised to see their bodies as an important aspect of their attractiveness. Whereas men generally see their bodies as objects to be built up, strengthened, used, and exercised, women are often horrified about developing muscles that will defeminize them, are afraid of strenuous activities, and are anxious about every little discomfort. Admittedly men carry their disregard for the limits of human strength to unreasonable lengths, but women too often carry their self-protectiveness beyond a healthy point. It seems that both sexes could learn a little from each other in this area.

As the weeks went on and the work became more frustrating, the women grew angrier and angrier. It took almost two months to get the house to the point where everyone could work on the aesthetic problems of their own rooms. The lack of gratification was difficult for the women to handle, even the Fresno women. Many of the new women had only worked on small projects before and were used to immediate results. The unrest among them grew. They began to talk about how Mimi and I were on "power trips," using them to gain some mysterious private glory. There were tears and accusations: "This

The first photograph in this section has never been reproduced before. It is a picture of the Cuntleaders, four of the Fresno students in their specially designed costumes doing cheers that celebrate female power. The young women created the activity and the costumes themselves, sometimes greeting visitors to our program at the airport, much to my chagrin. Although I loved it, I also felt embarrassed at such overt expression of womanly pride.

The other pictures present some of the performances and installations we developed at Fresno and/or for Womanhouse, one of the first public works of art to deal openly with female subject matter. During its month-long exhibition, Womanhouse was seen by more than nine thousand people. Since then, Womanhouse has inspired works of art around the world, and its themes provided the impetus for many women to begin creating art about their own experiences, which were validated by this early example of Feminist art.

The art created in Fresno, in Womanhouse and at Cal Arts, grew out of the principles of feminist art education as I developed them in the early seventies. These same ideas can be applied today in a variety of contexts: in women's art classes; in mixed classes (if male students are interested in a cooperative rather than competitive environment and are willing to alter their role-conditioned behavior patterns); in multicultural settings to help students reach personal subject matter. Feminist art education is content-oriented and dramatically different from most art education today, which generally focuses on aesthetic and career issues, rather than emphasizing the idea of art as the most profound expression of the human spirit.

OPPOSITE: Cuntleaders in their costumes performing cheers, Fresno, CA, 1970–71. (Photo courtesy Through the Flower Archives)

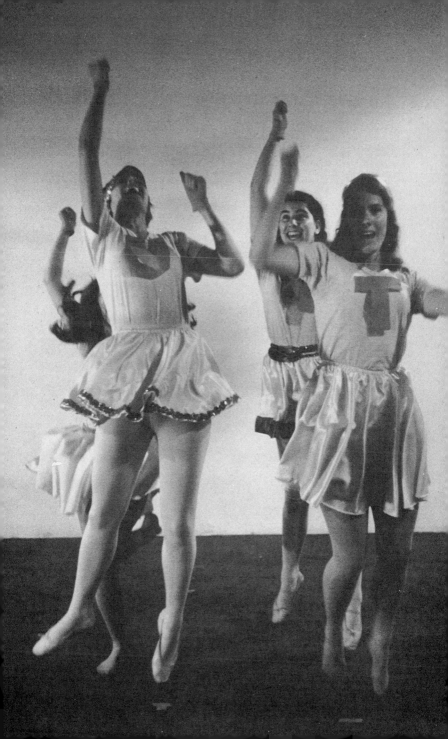

The performance *Three Women*, developed in the Feminist Art Program's Performance Group, was presented at *Womanhouse* by students Nancy Youdelman, Shawnee Wollenman, and Jan Oxenberg. The piece grew out of an informal session of role-playing. Excerpts from the monologues in the performance are included in the Appendix. (Photo courtesy Through the Flower Archives)

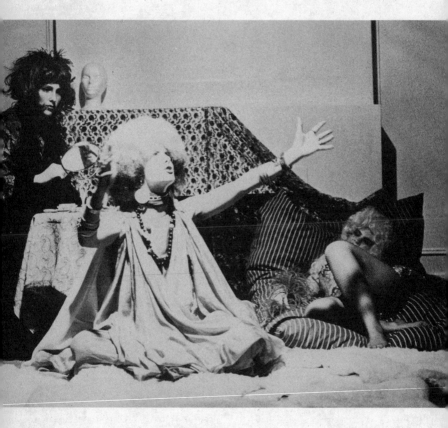

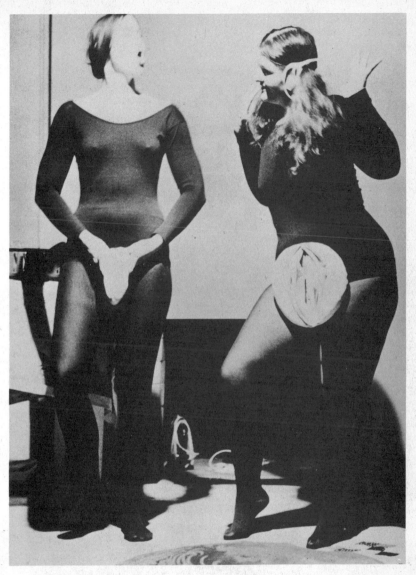

Faith Wilding and Jan Lester, students in the Feminist Art Program, performing Judy Chicago's *Cock and Cunt* play. The script is included in the Appendix. (Photo courtesy Through the Flower Archives)

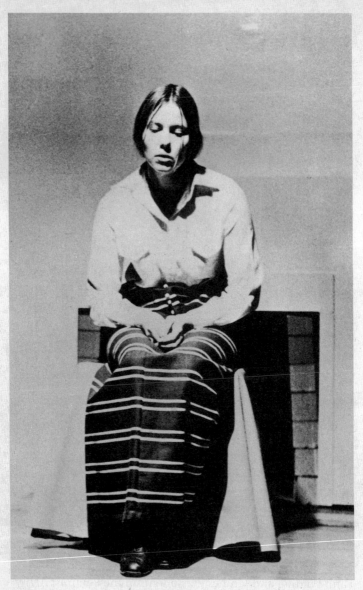

Waiting, written by Faith Wilding in 1971, was performed by Ms. Wilding at *Womanhouse. Waiting* is reprinted in its entirety in the Appendix. (Photo courtesy Through the Flower Archives)

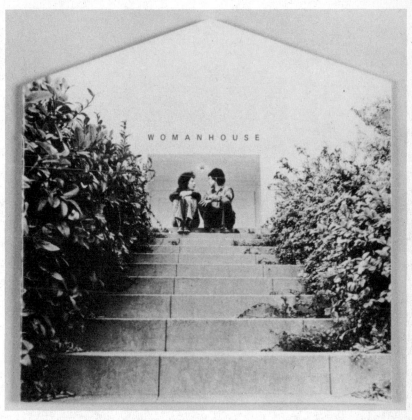

Womanhouse catalog, designed by Sheila de Brettville, with Miriam Schapiro and Judy Chicago, directors of the Feminist Art Program at the California Institute of the Arts, seated on the steps to the exhibition. (Photo: Donald Woodman)

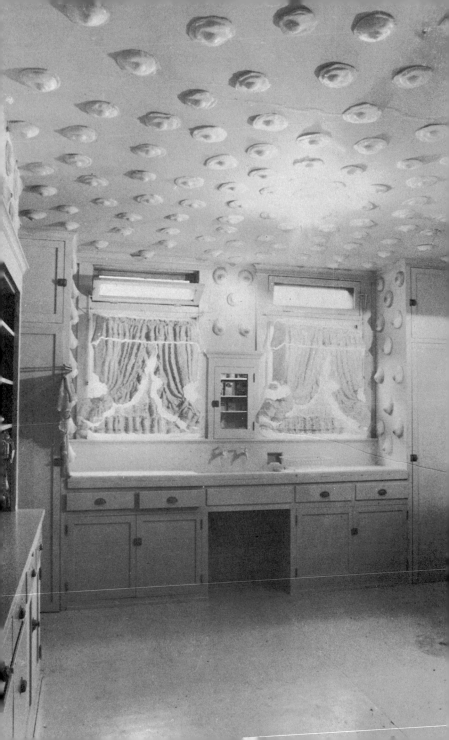

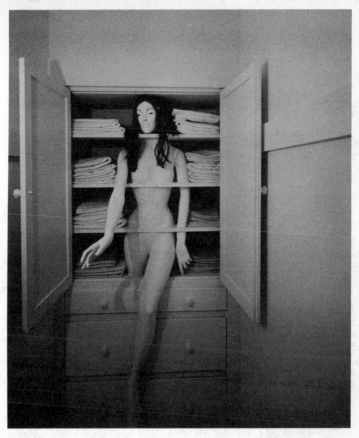

ABOVE: *Sheet Closet,* by student Sandra Orgel, contained not only varicolored sheets, but the image of a woman who, with the linens, was "closeted" within the confines of domestic role. (Photo courtesy Through the Flower Archives)

OPPOSITE: The *Nurturant Kitchen,* which was created by students Vickie Hodgetts, Robin Weltsch, and Susan Frazier in the Feminist Art Program, proved to be one of the most popular rooms in the house. A skin of fleshy-pink paint covered the walls, floors, and ceilings, as well as all of the objects and appliances. Plastic eggs that transmuted into breasts cascaded from the ceiling onto the walls, a metaphor for the kitchen as mother/nurturer. (Photo courtesy Through the Flower Archives)

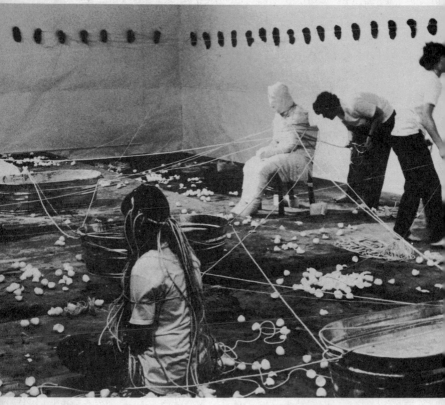

Ablutions was a performance piece conceived by me and several of my students, including Sandra Orgel, Aviva Ramani, and Suzanne Lacy, who later became an internationally known performance artist. In preparation for this work, I spent several days interviewing women who'd been raped. Their testimony was used on an audiotape that played continuously throughout this 1972 performance, which took place at the studio of a local artist. It was the first time the Los Angeles art community had ever been confronted with the reality of sexual violence, and the performance was met by stunned silence. (Photo courtesy Through the Flower Archives)

project is terrible. I'm not getting what I want from the program." "If we hadn't worked on this house, we could have been together. We're not together here. We're all working in our separate rooms. We're isolated" (this despite the continual collaborative work and the presence of twenty-three women every day in the same house). "I never do anything any more but work." "I thought that all women were equal. We're not all equal. You and Mimi have more authority than we do. Why do *you* get to make all the decisions?"

Our idea about dealing with problems in the context of a project was working all too well. The women were suffering from the results of the years in which too few demands were made upon them. They were used to a self-indulgent world, where they were rarely uncomfortable, always ready to give up if frustration became too much, never setting long-range goals or trying to do things that were far beyond their strength. There was a big confrontation. Why were they angry at Mimi and me, I asked? They should be angry at the society that had never demanded that they push beyond their limits, that they reach their potential, that they achieve something. They had joined the program of their own free will, because they wanted an opportunity to extend themselves beyond the limits that had been allowed them because they were women and assumed to be weak.

They were upset for two reasons: first, because demands were being made upon them to use muscles that were undeveloped or atrophied (both physically and emotionally) and, second, because many of them were unable to accept Mimi and me as authority figures. They had no models in their lives for women to be authorities on the basis of their accomplishments. The only female authorities in their lives were their mothers, and the young women had many unexpressed feelings toward them. Working with Mimi and me, they became confused. The rhetoric of the women's movement says that all women are equal, and so they are, on the basis of their humanity. But in reference to talents, abilities, and achievements, not everyone is equal. When women look around the world, they see that men are everywhere in positions of authority. When women encounter a woman as an authority figure, they can only imagine that she is like their own mothers. They try to lay their anger at their mothers upon them. The only alternative to seeing us as "mother authorities" that the women saw was that "all women should be equal." The problem with this in our program was that Mimi and I were artists, and the students wanted to learn what they could from us about being artists. Hence, we were authorities *in that situation*. (I wish to make a clear distinction between authority figures and authoritarianism, which is not at all what I mean. To be an authority figure in the sense that I use the term is to be an authority about a given subject and to have information that is valuable to others. This can be given without the misuse of power that so often characterizes male authority figures.)

The acceptance of women as authority figures or as role models is an important step in female education. If one sees a woman who has achieved, one can say: I'm like her. If she can do it, so can I. It is this process of identification, respect, and then self-respect that promotes growth. In struggling to separate Mimi and me from their mothers, the women were making a step toward accepting us as role models rather than as parents, against whose authority they would have to rebel. The ways the women had of dealing with us grew out of the parent-child relationship. Either they were children and we the parents—that is, they were powerless and subject to our control and we were powerful and almighty, or we were all the same, that is, siblings. This confusion indicates the level of development at which many women remain because they are always treated either as dependent children or as mothers. In emerging from that encapsulation, the women were able to see us more realistically, as people who knew something they wanted to know, but who could be challenged, criticized, and approached in a human way. By accepting the demands that we were placing upon them, they learned to place demands on themselves and then upon us for what they needed. Women are brought up to see men as the providers of their satisfactions and comforts and often do not know how to ask from themselves that which will give them real life satisfaction. Moreover, many women have internalized male attitudes and are afraid of women of ambition or strength, seeing them as monsters. In accepting the strength that Mimi and I had, they gave themselves permission to be strong and rejected the idea that there was something wrong with assertiveness, aggressiveness, and power if you were female.

Some of the anger and anxiety that was manifest during that period grew out of the fear that the house project would be a failure. The women didn't have the necessary confidence in themselves or in each other. Once, at a college where I was giving a workshop, I asked the women what they were most afraid of in working with other women, and they almost all replied: "that I'll be let down, disappointed," or "I can't trust women to come through." Many of the women went through a period similar to the one the previous year when I demanded that the women relate to me through their work. They made self-deprecating remarks, suddenly lost confidence in themselves, and worried incessantly about failing. When the house was nearing completion, their spirits rose and they began to see that their anxieties were unrealistic.

One thing that upset me greatly was that even the Fresno women, who had been through a similar period, became carried away in the frenzy of anger that overtook the women. I felt particularly hurt when they made accusations about my being on a "power" trip, I, who had worked so closely with them and given them so much of myself. But the process of female education was at work, a process that forces a confrontation between the developing women and the female figure who is placing demands upon them. At some point in the process, after the initial gratitude for the help, many women turn against this figure who has helped them. It's happened frequently in my years of working with women, and it always hurts.

As I became more aware of the patterns of behavior that each group went through, it became evident that this rejection mechanism happens when a woman feels that she is becoming stronger. One way of demonstrating that strength, which although negative is still an assertive act, is to reject the "mother" figure who helped her become strong. By saying "I don't need you any more," the woman feels a sense of power. Unfortunately, this need to feel powerful often results in hurting the very woman who made the growth possible. Instead of giving her back the love she provided, women sometimes feel a need to repudiate her and thus provide themselves with a false sense of independence, probably because their egos won't allow them to acknowledge their gratitude. Many strong women in the movement have been devastated by this dynamic of female growth. Only by understanding its dimension can we who are offering leadership protect ourselves against the terrible hurt of having a woman you've helped reward you with hate instead of love.

Just as the younger women went through this with me, Mimi and I went through the same process, although it was more complicated, because in some ways, she was more developed than I, and then I used her as a mother figure. In other ways, I was more realized than she, and she had to rely on me for growth. I think this might have been difficult for her, as she was sixteen years older than I, had a more established reputation as an artist, and was certainly more mature. As soon as we began to work together in Womanhouse, there began to be problems. She felt excluded from my closeness with the Fresno women. I wanted her to feel a part of what I had built, and so I withdrew from them in an attempt to make her feel more comfortable. She used to tell me things about myself with which I didn't agree. Her perceptions often didn't correspond to my own sense of myself, but I just went along with Mimi's criticisms, thinking that she knew more than I and that I should be open to her insights. If only I had challenged her when my perceptions differed from hers, but I needed her too much and was afraid that if I disagreed with her, she would reject me. It's interesting that my students probably had the same anxieties about me. We were *all* caught up in a process that none of us yet fully understood.

6

Womanhouse/ Performances

After the initial house repairs, the women turned their attention to the development of their individual projects. Some women worked alone, others collaborated. At no point did either Mimi or I dictate subject matter. In fact, the same thing happened that had taken place in Fresno. As soon as the constraints against working openly with female experience were lifted, ideas poured out. The rooms quickly took shape: One woman made a crocheted environment, another a lipstick bathroom, painted entirely red, walls, floors, bathtub, sink. Two women made a bridal staircase in which the bride was pictured, radiant and beautiful, at the top of the stairs, her train covering the carpet and going up the back of a mannequin who was attached to the bottom wall, headed into the obscurity of marriage and domestic life. One woman made a nursery in large scale that made adults feel like children again. There was a shoe closet, crammed full of shoes to match every conceivable outfit, and a private, personal space, all pink and soft and feminine, hidden inside a dirty, messy room.

Mimi was particularly interested in the potential of consciousness-raising for reaching subject matter for artmaking. We had tried a few sessions early in the year, and they proved valuable. Three of the women were working together in the kitchen and not having too much success. Mimi suggested that we try a consciousness-raising session on kitchens. As we went around the circle, women talked about their memories of the kitchens in their homes. It became clear that the kitchen was often the battlefield of the house. The giving and taking of food, what kind of food was fixed, who made food, and when it could and could not be eaten provided the means for a power struggle between mother and father, mother and children. The association of women with the kitchen and with the giving of food led to the idea of a nurturant kitchen, in which the walls, floors, and objects were covered with a flesh-colored skin, and plastic eggs transmuting into breasts cascaded down from the ceiling onto the walls. Room after room took shape until the house became a total environment, a repository of female experience and womanly dreams.

Womanhouse provided a context for work that both in technique and in content revealed female experience. There were quilts and curtains, sewn sculptures, bread-dough pieces, and a crocheted room. Several women artists from the community contributed work to the house, which provided their work with new meaning. Wanda Westcoast placed her plastic formed curtains in the kitchen. They were more understandable there than when they were first shown in a clean, white art gallery, where there was little understanding of art that grows out of women's perceptions of reality. The upstairs hallway was hung with quilts by a Los Angeles quiltmaker, whose work was not even considered art until then. Womanhouse became both an environment that housed the work of women artists working out of their own experiences and the "house" of female reality into which one entered to experience the real facts of women's lives, feelings, and concerns.

In Fresno, we had discovered that something quite profound occurred when people came into our studio. Because the studio had been built on the basis of the needs and values of women, the environment reflected a very particular kind of reality, one that grew out of the personality structures of women. In our studio, we demanded direct exposure of feelings, honest self-revelation, and a breakdown of rigid role-playing. Student, teacher, visitor, famous artist, department chairman, all were asked to relinquish their "status" or role and relate entirely on a human level, to be open and expressive in response to our directness. Our environment reflected our values, the ones this society encourages women to adopt: openness, vulnerability, caring for others, and placing the needs of people above the rigid rules of institutions or academic disciplines. One might ask: Aren't you just prolonging women's oppression by being what society has made us? The answer to that was clear to all of us. It seems to me that growth takes place by starting where we really are and moving on. We women have spent much of our time hiding who we are, because we have been made to feel ashamed. The program made it possible for all of us to be ourselves and to show others who we were, in our actions and in our art. We carried the values of our female orientation into our artmaking and quite naturally made art that used form primarily as a way of making the content evident, and not as an issue in itself. Out of this process grew Womanhouse and personal growth for all those involved.

When people came into Womanhouse, they reacted in several ways. Many women immediately felt comfortable in a reality they intuitively understood and to which they could easily respond. Some women, particularly those who had accepted certain masculine values having to do with toughness, lack of emotional expression, and the idea that women's experiences are inherently trivial, were hesitant in their responses. On the one hand, they were touched by the ambiance; on the other hand, they were frightened by its implication in terms of their lives and their relationships with men who could never take women seriously. Some men felt uncomfortable, at least during their first exposure to what was for them a totally unfamiliar world. They did not understand the rules of our world and had as little cultural preparation for our openly emotional expressiveness as most of us did for their machines, tools, and emotional restraint. The most shocking aspect of the experience of Womanhouse for men had to do with a sense of not being in control. Men are generally encouraged by the culture to take control of life situations and often develop a tendency to "have to be" in control all the time. In Womanhouse, they were spectators to *our* lives, to *our* art, to *our* point of view, just as we had been the spectators to male activities for centuries. This made them the "other" instead of us. Whatever prejudices men had toward women, they brought them to Womanhouse and interpreted it accordingly. For example, one man thought the house was a wonderful parody on women, despite the fact that there was nothing but compassion and empathy in the whole evironment. I pointed out to him that it was *he* who saw women's lives, concerns, and paraphernalia as amusing, and that he was not seeing Womanhouse at all, only his own attitudes. In struggling to see our work as we saw it, men were forced to struggle to see us as we saw ourselves, rather than as they saw us in their fantasized, socially reinforced concepts of women.

For some men, this was profoundly liberating, educational, and revelatory. Never before had they had the opportunity to see women's lives from women's point of view and to be momentarily released from the often burdensome sense of responsibility imposed upon them by the male role. The initial sense of threat frequently changed into real fascination with experiences and feelings they knew little about but were able to perceive through our art. For men whose identity was deeply invested in male role-playing and masculine dominance, the whole environment was so threatening that they could not even begin to relate to the work as art. However, if men related to it, that was fine, but it was to a female audience that the house was directed, that audience that the women's movement gave birth to, and it was to women that we listened in terms of evaluations and criticisms and responses. As one woman said, it was the first work of art she had ever seen that she completely understood. Although female art certainly has the potential of changing men's attitudes toward women, I believe that the first responsibility of women today, both in and out of the arts, has to be to women. If Womanhouse affected men, that was all to the good, but most of all, Womanhouse was important because it was a step toward building an art that allowed women to feel that their lives had meaning, that their experiences were rich, and that they had something of value to contribute to the world as women.

For me, the response to Womanhouse was a revelation. During the month that it was open, almost ten thousand people came to see it, mostly through word of mouth. I had sensed that the direct revelation of female experience could have a profound impact upon the culture, but to think that and to see it actualized were two different things. I was still unsure about my own direction and had been very busy since my return to Los Angeles with Womanhouse, my book, and various other activities aimed at the development of a female art community. I had also involved myself quite deeply in the Program's Performance Workshop, the results of which had been very important in the impact of Womanhouse. This had given me the opportunity to test out my desires to do theater as a way of expressing those aspects of myself that I didn't see how to bring into my art. In Fresno, when I worked with the women in performance, I had discovered that I had a gift for directing. When I was a child, I performed plays on the back porch in which I "directed" all the children in the neighborhood. Womanhouse provided me with the opportunity to try out this talent again to see whether performance might not be a better place for my energies than painting.

A number of the women in the program were interested in extending the impact of the house through the use of performance, feeling that the experience of being in a female environment would be even greater if performance were used in conjunction with the visual works. We formed a performance group and used the living room of Womanhouse as our theater. There was a central performance space, and the audience was seated on the floor around that space. Usually, it was so crowded during the performances that the spectators and actresses were no more than a foot apart. While the house was still being repaired, a number of us began to meet regularly at my home to develop pieces that would relate to the rest of the environment and provide a clearer sense of the entrapment that the house meant for many women. I worked in the group both as the informal group leader and as a group member.

We started by "playing around." Our experiments grew out of our ability as women to put out direct feeling. We cried, groaned, screamed, made animal noises, always trying to focus on a feeling and connect with it and with each other. Once, spontaneously, two of the women lined us up and began to inspect us as men inspect women. They looked us up and down, choosing several of us to stand on chairs, meant to be auction blocks. Then they proceeded to comment on the physical faults the women had, intuitively focusing on these things that had plagued them all their lives: fat thighs, acne, bulging stomachs. The initiators of the piece had struck at the self-consciousness we all felt about our bodies. We thought the piece as it evolved was good, but decided not to perform it because we felt unsure about performing pieces in front of men that involved body exposure, which this piece did. We talked about performing it only for female audiences, and everyone agreed to that. The performance stimulated a long discussion about the problems of performing pieces involving nudity. We all felt that men, at this point in history, couldn't see women's bodies objectively, and that, in order to discourage sexist perception, we should be very careful in our use of body exposure if we intended to perform for mixed audiences.

One night, we all lay down on the floor and began pretending we were in labor. We lay on our back, legs spread, crying: "Puu-uu-uush, puu-uu-uush," until we were all laboring together, pushing together, until we felt this strong emotional connection with each other and with all women who

had ever borne children. One of the women became upset
and began to cry hysterically. Everyone comforted her, a pro-
cedure we had developed to handle the frequent expressions
of feeling that occurred in the group. The experience had
called up memories of being born and then abandoned by her
mother. We began talking about that, and it seemed that all
of us carried around a sense of never having been nurtured
enough. We began to play with that feeling, crawling around
on our hands and knees, eyes closed, like infants, crying
"Mommy, mommy, mommy." As women made contact with
the feelings of longing inside them, we decided to develop a
performance that would deal with birth, nurturing and fulfillment. At first, we thought that we would pick out members of the audience and "mother" them, rock them, and comfort them. We discussed the work of the Living Theatre,
which had audience/players confrontation. We all felt that
there was something inherently dishonest about that, because
there was "symbolic contact," but after the performance
there was nothing real left. We decided instead to "mother"
each other, hoping to generate a longing for comfort and
contact in the audience, that longing that most people put
away as being childish. We worked at feeling and then projecting the sense of connection that we experienced in "mothering" each other. We held each other in our arms, rocking
back and forth, crooning softly. The *Birth Trilogy* developed
out of these sessions.

It was a three-part piece. In the first part, six women stood
in a line, legs spread, bodies close together, arms around each
other's waists. Slowly, they began to push down with their
legs, making them into a birth passage, through which the
last woman in line was pushed, propelled by the thrusting
legs of the other women. After three "babies" had been born,

the three women playing "babies" lay down on the floor while the three other women sat down back to back. Then, the "babies" slowly crawled to the "mother" figures, who embraced them, rocked them, comforted them, and nurtured them. The third part was called "Wailing." All six women knelt on the floor, heads together and arms around each other, forming a kind of dome shape with their bodies. One of the women began to hum, a slow, haunting melody. The other women joined in, and the humming became louder and louder, more and more rhythmic. The sound was like the danger cry made by Algerian and Tunisian women, and as it reached a higher and higher intensity, became the sound of orgasm, of labor, of joy, of ecstasy.

Sometime after we performed this piece, I did a workshop with a number of women at an eastern college. I showed them some of the work being done by women in the program, had a consciousness-raising session, and then, on the second day, worked with them in performance, which none of them had ever done. There were twenty-six women in the group. I divided them into groups of five or six and asked them to invent pieces spontaneously, which they did. Then we formed one long line and did the birth piece, birthing all twenty-six women. At first the women giggled, trying to protect themselves against the feeling that was growing in the room. Slowly, they began to take that feeling seriously, to honor it, and in so doing to honor themselves and their own very special capacity to project emotion directly in ways that men know little about. The same thing happened that day that happened in Fresno and in the performance workshop. The women felt themselves and each other "as women, doing something together that women do," and it created enormous excitement. That afternoon, those women "plugged into themselves" and into their energy sources, an essential step in human and creative development. I have found that when women who are educated begin to express their feelings as women, emotion and intellect merge to make a greater expressiveness than most men are now capable of.

One evening, in the performance workshop, we all dressed up, making up our faces, putting on wigs and outlandish costumes. Immediately, the room was transformed into a brothel, as if the act of self-decoration was seen as it really is, a kind of prostitution of the self to gain male approval. We related to each other "through" our roles, and out of that evening grew a piece called *Three Women,* based on the autobiographies of three women in the group. Each of them had reached crossroads in their lives when they had to make decisions about being "women" in the sense that society demanded, or defying society and being themselves. They had all made healthy choices, but it was easy for them to imagine what would have happened to them if they had accepted society's commands. Out of this imaginary projection came three characters: Sparkyl, the proverbial "whore with the heart of gold"; Rainbow, the hippie chick, who deluded herself that she could escape the damage men inflict upon women by "putting out good vibrations"; and Roslyn, who took care of men, no matter how they hurt her, because she felt that men were too helpless to survive without the support of women. In this piece, we tried to let the real human pain and suffering come through the "roles" the women had adapted. Women's masochism was also dealt with in this piece, inasmuch as the women participated in their own victimization by the choices they made, by "mothering" men, by allowing themselves to be seen as objects, and by living in fantasy.

We had developed a group process to invent and work on

pieces. As a piece grew out of one of the informal performances, we would all work on it until we felt ready to perform
it. Then we would work together, rehearsing it, improving it.
We all took turns acting, directing, costuming, and stage
managing. Sometimes, one or another of the women had a
clear idea for a piece or for the subject matter for a piece, as
Faith Wilding did when she said she wanted to do a theater
piece about female passivity.

Faith and I went to a friend's house for dinner. While
there, we began talking about Faith's piece and her ideas.
Soon we were writing down all the things we had ever waited
for in our lives, particularly in adolescence, when we "waited
for boys to call, waited for boys to ask us to dance," waited
for boys to take the initiative in just about everything, never
daring to ask a boy out for fear of being thought "unfemi-
nine." Faith took the long list home with her and worked on
it, bringing it back to the performance workshop, where we
went over it, working on the lines, the emotional tone, and
the rhythm until the piece felt right to all of us. The fact that
we all exchanged roles provided a fluid working situation
and meant that everyone had a chance to express herself.
Sometimes several women would try a role until we found the
one who was best suited for it.

The other pieces that we performed were: the *Cock and
Cunt* play, written in Fresno by me, in a fit of passion, but so
appropriate to the house that we all felt it should be included,
and two maintenance pieces, in which a woman ironed a
sheet and another scrubbed the floor. It was interesting to
note how the audience responded, particularly to the ironing
piece. Some nights, everyone would be bored and agitated
and start talking, as if to try to drown out the sight from their
mind. In other nights, the audience sat there, rapt and still,

silent throughout the piece. Sometimes people ran out, angry that they should have to watch a woman iron, unwilling to look at what women really do with their time.

On the first night that Womanhouse was open, we performed only for women. The response was overwhelming. The actresses could hardly get through the lines of the *Cock and Cunt* play (a comedy), the laughter and applause were so loud. During the *Three Women* piece, women cried, laughed, and empathized, and the *Waiting* play caused a profound silence—everyone was deeply moved. After the performances, the acting group was ecstatic, and our ecstasy lasted until our next performance the following week, which was for a mixed audience. Throughout the evening, there was inappropriate silence, embarrassed laughter or muffled applause. We couldn't believe it. I was so depressed that I wanted to run away and hide. Later that evening when I was riding in the car with Lloyd, I began to express my distress. He listened to my ranting and raving about how the men hated the performances and how we should never perform for mixed audiences because the women saw the pieces through the eyes of the men and couldn't respond directly, and on and on. Lloyd had been there, and he said that he felt that that was not at all what had happened. Rather, he perceived that many of the men were so overwhelmed by the experience of the house and the performances that they didn't know *how* to respond. They were receiving new information, information that they had never known or suspected about women's feelings and experiences. Lloyd felt that the men in the audience were not so much hostile as unknowing. I thought about that and even talked to some men who had come to the performances and it turned out that, by and large, Lloyd was right. Unfortunately, because of the ambivalence of men's responses, many women were caught between identifying with their own responses to the work and that of their men. This contributed to the sense of suppressed feeling that was evident in mixed audiences. Certainly there were men who didn't like the house or the performances or anything we had done. But there were other men who responded deeply, but who didn't know how to show their response. Many men, accustomed to images of women that were quite different from those we presented, felt somewhat shocked by the new information they were receiving about women and women's point of view. For it has been woman's artificial self, not her real self, with which most men have been familiar.

> She was like an actress who must compose a face, an attitude to meet the day. . . . She must redesign the face, smooth the anxious brows, separate the crushed eyelashes, wash off the traces of secret, interior tears, accentuate the mouth as upon a canvas, so it will hold its luxuriant smile. Inner chaos, like those secret volcanoes which suddenly lift the neat furrows of a peacefully plowed field, awaited behind all disorders of face, hair and costume, for a fissure through which to explode.[1]

In her novel *A Spy in the House of Love,* Anaïs Nin describes Sabina, a woman who continually "acts," trying on one role after another. She is all women who "play roles" that men have written: mother, temptress, ingenue, child/woman, goddess. Beneath the costumed, bedecked, and altered self that Sabina presented to the world, she was in a boiling rage that she could never be herself. Sabina might be

[1] Anaïs Nin, *A Spy in the House of Love* (New York: Bantam Books, Inc., 1968), pp. 6–7.

seen as a symbol for many women, who, trapped in female role and enraged at their entrapment, still are unable to break out. (One might note that men play roles too, but that the roles allowed them are less inconsistent with the range of their humanity than are those roles traditionally seen as female.) When given the opportunity to express their real feelings in the program, it was interesting that the women's first expressions were of rage. They began to "act out" all of the brutalization they had experienced. Performance seemed to provide the most direct means of expressing anger, and perhaps that is why it proved so valuable in the program. Women's anger against female roles and against men has been turned inward in an internalized self-hate that has left many women riddled with anguish, filled with self-loathing, and afraid to express their real feelings. As George Eliot said through the character of Madame Deronda, in 1876, in *Daniel Deronda:*

> You are not a woman. You may try—but you can never imagine what it is to have a man's force of genius in you, and yet to suffer the slavery of being a girl. To have a pattern cut out—this is the . . . woman; this is what you are wanted for; a woman's heart must be of such a size and no larger, else it must be pressed small, like Chinese feet. . . .

The compression of human personality creates anger, and if that anger is not expressed, it turns in upon itself, diminishing the personality into a state of nonbeing, nonacting, passivity. Although women are allowed emotional expressiveness, they often do not have access to their feelings because of blocked anger. Men learn, from early boyhood, to use their fists to express their rage or to channel their anger into so-

cially acceptable avenues like combative sports, social and
business competition, and war—sometimes even in sex. Although these are often profoundly unhealthy methods for expressing anger and cost men a large part of their humanity,
and although many men suffer from unexpressed anger, men
do have more methods for expressing rage than women. Anger can be extremely productive and healthy: anger against
one's limits, against oppression, against the facts of the human
condition. This anger can lead to creative growth. Women are
made to feel guilty about any direct expression of anger. We
are not allowed physical expression of anger, have few socially
accepted outlets, and when we try to express anger verbally,
we are accused of being "bitches" or "loudmouths." We are
allowed only covert displays of anger: silence, passive with-
drawal, manipulative behavior, covert action, and the use of
"feminine wiles." Women, prohibited from the direct expression of anger, are thereby also denied the creative aspects of
anger.

One of the reasons performance proved to be so important
in the program is that it provided a release for debilitating,
unexpressed anger, thereby opening up the whole range of
emotions for creative work. The symbolic expression of anger
fits in well with women's acculturated personality structures,
as anger is not exactly the same force in women that it is in
men. Because we have not been encouraged to "act out" anger in physical ways, there is little developed connection in
our emotional structures between rage and physical violence.
Thus, once in an environment that accepted the expression of
anger as natural, women found it quite easy to release their
rage symbolically, through performances. This allowed the
women to work through many feelings that had previously
immobilized them. For example, in the early sessions in

Fresno, when the women "acted out" walking down the street and being accosted by men, everyone seemed able to play the male role. They could "take on" the characteristics, the tough swagger, of men "coming on." It was as if they knew the words so well: "Hey baby, how about it? We-ee, what a fox. Sweetheart, you wanna fuck?" All the women seemed to feel an enormous sense of relief after that session, as if by characterizing men, they gained some control in a situation that had always seemed beyond control.

Often, after the initial release obtained through performance sessions, women moved into other areas of artmaking, using the ideas they had touched on in performance as the stimuli for paintings, sculptures, and films. The artmaking process then allowed a wide range of expressive possibilities, but only after blocked anger was released through performance. Other women became interested in the potential for changing values implied in the informal performance techniques we were exploring. Because women have so rarely revealed their real feelings as women in their artmaking, there was a level of intense shock at the revelation of female experience in the performances. It wasn't until we saw how audiences responded to the performances that any of us realized that we had stumbled upon an important technique for changing values.

Margaret Sanger, in her autobiography, discussed the impact upon a congressman of a letter sent by one of his female constituents. The letter described the suffering the woman endured because she had no access to birth-control information, the dissemination of which was still a crime sixty years ago. Her story was so moving that the congressman, previously resistant to all facts and figures presented to him and adamant in his refusal to support birth control, abruptly changed his position. This is an example of the fact that men are often responsive to women only on a one-to-one basis, while remaining unresponsive to the needs and feelings of women on a social level. In the bedroom, hidden from the sight of their male peers, many men allow themselves to be vulnerable and receptive to a woman. Even the most defensive man, faced with the unhappiness of a woman he cares about, often feels compelled to act privately in ways that he would never admit to publicly. It is within the bedroom walls that the intimate contact, struggles, and violence of man/woman relationships are played out, often with the illusion that the struggle is peculiar to that particular couple.

Feminist thinking has illuminated the fact that we are all conditioned by society to "play" the parts of male and female as dictated by the culture. Within male role-playing, there have been avenues for the expression of the male point of view toward the female, toward the world, and toward himself. Our traditions in art contain the perceptions of men, but nowhere in Western culture are women's perceptions symbolized in a coherent set of images. It is always a man who embodies the human condition. From *Hamlet* to *Waiting for Godot*, the struggles of humanity are embodied in male characters, created by men, reflecting themselves and each other. Women, prohibited by law and by social taboo from revealing their true perception, can only now even think about portraying men as *they* see them, thereby providing for men a mirror that shows them new aspects of themselves. I think that the reason our performances in Fresno and at Womanhouse created so much tension, excitement, and response was that we told the truth about our feelings as women in them. Because performance can be so direct, because we were developing our performances from a primitive, gut level, we articulated feelings that had simply never been so openly expressed in artmaking. Although many women in the arts have struggled to give voice to their experiences as women, their forms, like mine, have been so transposed (into the language of sophisticated artmaking) that the content could be ignored by a culture that doesn't understand or accept the simplest facts of women's lives, much less subtle and transformed imagery. We learned a profound lesson about aesthetic perception (particularly in men) when in Fresno, the chairman of the art department, a sophisticated, liberal man, came to visit our studio. He saw an environment by Faith Wilding, a piece that dealt with the sacrifice of the female by male culture. It was a religious piece, implying crucifixion, death, and destruction, and the symbolism was very overt. Hanging around the walls were bloody Kotexes, which he perceived as "white material with red spots," so disassociated was he from the ability to perceive content or to recognize anything that did not grow out of *his* cultural experience. If a man like that, educated in art language, cannot recognize a bloody Kotex, or understand a not very subtle work of art, how can he be expected to respond to any art work that relates *in any way* to female experience or differs from male cultural references to any degree?

What this suggests is that the cultural gap between men and women at this moment in history is almost unimaginable. Women in the arts, in the professions, in the academies, blinded by the illusion of equality, are just beginning to grasp how profoundly alienated women and men really are. As we move out of the historical time when men were the primary breadwinners and women were confined to procreative and domestic functions, we are left with a heritage of social roles and attitudes that are entirely inconsistent with reality but that assert their hold on us nonetheless. The problems women face in achieving equality are primarily problems of values, values that keep us subject even if we "open doors." Our subjugation is psychological and our "otherness" the result of cultural differences between us and men so profound as to sometimes make it seem that we are members of different species. How can these differences be overcome, so that men and women can reach across the culture gap?

> The gap between male and female . . . is not a universal constant, but rather the distance between public and private that developed with the first industrial revolution. . . . Today the hemisphere of the public has been assigned to the male and the hemisphere of the private to the female. Each sex has become a symbol for its territory. The conflict between them can then be seen as a reflection of the longing of each to be part of the other's sphere, to link the public with the private in our schizoid world, to embrace the whole of life.[2]

When we performed, the audience was usually shocked, then fascinated by the fact that we were bringing the "private" sphere into the light, making the private public, and in so doing, taking a large step toward bridging the culture chasm between men and women. Because women have always taken responsibility for the private in life, men have been totally relieved of that responsibility. Not only do women have to move into public life, but men have to share the burdens of private life before any real change can take place. This means that men have to be educated emotionally, and the first step

[2] Nancy Reeves, *Womankind* (Chicago: Aldine-Atherton, Inc., 1971), p. 29.

in that education is to be made to "see" women, to feel with us, experience our point of view.

The view from the private world is considerably different from the view from the public perspective. By bringing the private into public view, women bring the deepest level of psychic reality out of the bedroom, and in this case, onto the stage, where culture itself can be confronted, rather than a single male representative of that culture, as in heterosexual relationships where one woman struggles with one man. Some men have responded to our performances by calling them "therapy," in an effort to discredit them as art. This reflects the total schizophrenia of male culture, which has taught us all to believe that authentic feeling must be restricted to the therapist's office or to the bedroom. To express feeling is to be "womanly," and if we want to change the values of this culture, we must educate the entire society to appreciate rather than denigrate "womanliness" in art and in life.

In order for this to be accomplished, men's damage must be exposed, faced, altered. Men must be helped to feel again, and the point of greatest disjuncture in male personalities is pivoted upon their sense of "difference" from and "superiority" to women. When we brought men into *our* environment, Womanhouse, our studio, our performances, we brought them into an unfamiliar world, where their only guides were their feelings, a part of themselves as atrophied as our muscles for assertion and independence. Too often, men are unable to comprehend the world with their "gut" and instead judge, objectify, and abstract information. In dealing with ourselves as women and making art aimed first at women, we were violating role definition and pleasing each other rather than men—that is, we were "being independent." In so doing, and in letting men be the observers to our independence, we forced them to be independent emotionally and thus to face their own damaged abilities. It was only in that kind of situation that men could make an empathetic identification with the despair we feel about *our* damage. As long as we go to men, move into their sphere without demanding that they move into ours simultaneously, we will always be at a disadvantage, we will always be the "other" in their world. What we glimpsed in our performances was the opportunity to make men feel themselves "other" and thereby force them to identify with us on a psychic level. It is not enough for us to learn to identify with men; we have done that all our lives. *Men have to learn to identify with us,* and it is this process that feminist performance and feminist art can promote, particularly if they exist on a wide scale throughout the country. Womanhouse and the performances we did there helped me clarify the possible relationship between women's art and the culture at large. I wondered if there was a way for abstract art to have the same kind of impact on values that the representational art and performances of Womanhouse had provided.

Finding My Way and Discovering Women's Art

Early in the fall of 1971, shortly after my return from Fresno, I went to visit Anaïs Nin. I met Anaïs at a social gathering and she told me that she had read and liked one of the articles I wrote for the *Everywoman* issue on the Fresno program. When I went to her house, it was a warm day. She had asked me to lunch and I was hungry. When I arrived, she offered to make me an omelet but expressed disinterest in food herself. Since she was one of my heroines, I felt embarrassed to sit there while she cooked for me, so I declined her offer. In the next few hours, while we were engaged in an intense and rewarding discussion, she asked me several times if I'd like to eat. Each time, I asked her if she was hungry, and when she said "no," I quickly replied, "Well, I'm not hungry either."

Finally, by three o'clock, faint with appetite, I accepted her offer of orange juice. Anaïs squeezed a glass of juice for me on one of those old-fashioned juicers, the kind that requires a lot of wrist action. I watched her hands twisting the oranges and thought: "Oh, no, *she* shouldn't be squeezing orange juice for *me, I* should be doing something for *her.* After all, *those hands* are the ones that wrote all those great books." After a while, I got over my awe of her, but the visit had a big impact on me. We discussed the confusion I felt about what direction I wanted to pursue in my work. I explained that I felt as if all these new possibilities had opened up for me as a result of the women's movement. Since I had become involved in the movement, I had, in addition to painting and teaching, lectured, started working in performance, and made some films. I told her that I felt as if my art was not reflecting my whole self and that I thought that the best thing I could do would be to give up painting and become involved in some other artmaking method.

She suggested that I use writing to "try out" all the various paths I could see myself taking and as a method of exploring the many directions for the arts that feminist consciousness seemed to suggest. She said that writing allowed one to "act out" what one could not actually live out. I went home determined to work on a book based upon my experiences and struggles. But I was frightened at the prospect. People in the past had told me that I *could* write, but I never believed them. I think that I had difficulty absorbing the idea of being able to write along with being able to paint. An "artist," I had learned, was generally mute and inarticulate. It was difficult to put together the fact that I was visually talented, could "direct," perform, organize, speak publicly, teach, and now, according to Anaïs, write, too. But I figured if anyone should know if someone could write, she should. However, just trying to be an artist had resulted in men saying I couldn't be an artist and a woman too. How could I be an artist and a writer and an organizer and a performer/director, a teacher, a politically active person, and a woman also? Was it all right to be all those things, I wondered? And how could I either integrate my talents or choose among them?

Working on the book helped me to organize my thoughts and ideas and to examine the experiences I had been having. While I was writing it, I also began experimenting with overtly feminist visual images. About the same time that I visited Anaïs, I started working at a print shop owned by a well-established male artist. He had always been very supportive of me and had offered me a chance to make a lithograph. (I must say, at this point, that although I did meet with a great deal of rejection from the male world, there were always a few people who supported me. These included, in addition to Lloyd, several other male artists; my first dealer, whose gallery unfortunately had closed by 1967; and a husband-and-wife collecting team in Los Angeles, without whom much of my work would never have been made. But although I received a level of support, it was a hard battle for me to feel that I could really be myself without losing that help.)

The lithograph I made was inspired by a conversation I had had at a friend's house. Four of us, all women in our early thirties, were discussing menstruation. Suddenly we realized that none of us had ever openly discussed that subject in any depth before. As we were all involved in art, that realization led us to a conversation about the absence of menstruation images in art and literature made by women. I decided to do a menstruation lithograph, called "Red Flag." It was an image of a woman's hand pulling a bloody Tampax out of her vagina. I tried to make the image as overt as I could, and even then some people interpreted the Tampax as a bloody penis, a testament to the damage done to our perceptual powers by the absence of images of female reality.

Working on the print was a real experience. I was very nervous when I brought the photograph to the litho shop, where I was to work with a male printer. I didn't know how he would react, and I was still extremely uncomfortable about exposing my point of view as a woman around men. Working on the print helped me considerably. The printer and I calmly talked about adjusting the blood color and making sure that the Tampax looked like it was really emerging from the vagina. I made the print for two reasons: first, I wanted to validate female subject matter by using a "high art" process, which is what hand lithography is, and second, I think I was trying to test male reaction to overt female subject matter. In fact, as I think back about the eight months after I returned from Fresno, I can see that I was actively testing my limits and my talents, was searching for a method of integrating my art and my feminism, and was also trying to gauge the potential response of the established art community to the new work I was making. Having internalized so many taboos throughout the years, I was sure that people would have violent reactions to the print. However, if the printer or people in the shop had any difficulty in dealing with the image, their professionalism never let them demonstrate it. I can see now that I was slowly developing the confidence that I could, in fact, reveal my real feelings in my work and that nothing terrible would happen.

After I made the Tampax litho, I brought it home and looked at it. I hung it in the same room as "Desert Fan," which was one of the paintings I had made in Fresno. I looked at both of them for a long time. "Desert Fan" was beautiful, but its content was submerged. "Red Flag" was clear in its content but it did not possess the layers of meaning that the "Fan" painting had. Could I get these two things together? I was still sure that I would have to stop making paintings like the "Fans" and the "Pasadena Lifesavers." The Tampax litho made me see that I *could* make work whose subject matter was clear. But what did that piece and later, the "Menstruation Bathroom" in Womanhouse have to do with my abstract work? Before I reached any conclusions, Womanhouse had opened and I had gotten caught up in the performance program.

By the time Womanhouse closed, I had finished the first draft of my book, seen the positive responses to both Womanhouse and my print, and in the process developed greater ease about expressing my own point of view. I realized that the reason I had thought about doing performance was that I wanted my work to have the same *impact* on values that performance seemed able to produce. Trying it helped me see that even though performance did offer the opportunity to express female subject matter more directly than did abstract art, I was a sophisticated artist. This meant that I would only be satisfied if I could do "high quality theater" and that would require that I develop a whole range of skills which I did not have. It would be quite different to develop a real feminist theater than to do simple and relatively uncomplicated performance pieces.

I had been drawing and painting since I was three years old. All those years had been spent developing keen visual abilities. I would have to start all over again if I were to do theater. Suddenly, that struck me as ridiculous. Why should I relinquish the skills I already had? I discovered then that I didn't *want* to repudiate the aesthetic tradition in which I

was raised, albeit male, or pretend that my skills and sophistication were something to be devalued and discarded as
"male," "elitist," or "bourgeois." Rather, I wanted to wed my
skills to my real ideas and to aspire to the making of art that
could clearly reveal my values and point of view as a woman.

I recognized that I could not and did not want to graft
some other stylistic method onto what had been the slow,
steady process of my artmaking life. Even though younger
women were going to be able to build their art directly out of
their experiences as women, something that I had not been
able to do, that did not mean that I could not make my art
reflect *my* experiences. I was thirty-three years old. I had
come full circle. I had examined my life, my goals, my aspirations, my decisions, and I decided that I did not *have* to
abandon my artmaking process. Rather, I had to accept my
own experience, find a way to integrate it into my art, and
put my skills to work *expressing,* rather than hiding, my real
feelings.

I decided, in that spring of 1972, to go back to my studio to
begin a series of drawings, to find a way back to myself and
my life as an artist that I had had to interrupt for eight
months. Starting to work again was a revelation, for I had
changed and grown in that time away from my studio. I now
knew what my goal was: to make my form language reflect
my real feelings as a woman, a goal that I am now, in 1974,
beginning to realize. Then, I slowly and haltingly began to try
to make my subject matter clearer. I used the form language I
had spent ten years in developing to express my longing to
grow and my acceptance that my childhood was over—childhood, the time when all things are possible because one is still
unformed.

In the spring of 1972, another event occurred that forced

me to face the end of my childish dreams of escaping responsibility, being twenty again, and being "taken care of" by a mother figure. After a series of unfortunate misunderstandings between us, Mimi decided to withdraw from most of our activities together. She remained committed only to the Feminist Art Program, preferring to end her involvement in all the other aspects of the female art community we had been building. I was devastated. I felt as though I had lost the love I needed. I didn't understand why she had decided to so drastically alter our relationship. I felt rejected. I felt punished and again, when I didn't know where else to go with my feelings, I went deeper into my studio life.

I made a series of drawings structured on a grid that Mimi had used. I guess that by adopting her format, I tried to hold onto her a little longer. Even while I was going through the feelings, I knew that they were out of proportion to reality. All that had happened was that a friend of mine had, for her own reasons, decided to change certain aspects of her life. In so doing, she changed our relationship, which I didn't like. But for me it had mythic meaning, in the sense that she had represented the "mother" who would love me for being independent, something that I wanted as much as any student in the program or woman in the society. That want, which, in my estimation, most women share, is not a function of having had "bad" mothering. Rather it is a result of growing up in a male-dominated society, in which women condition their daughters toward behavior that is "safe" and therefore unchallenging to male domination. To have a mother who loves you for being independent is to have a mother who fosters rebellion in your heart and revolution in your bones. And that can only come to pass in a feminist community.

When Mimi withdrew her "mothering" from me, I felt

alone and frightened. I did not know if I could continue my fight against the culture. I didn't want the responsibility alone, as I had not wanted it before. But now I felt I had no choice. I either had to retreat into a more private and personal sphere or I had to go on by myself. I can see now that a split between Mimi and me was inevitable, especially after we brought the Feminist Art Program to the building in which Cal Arts was actually housed. The Fresno program was away from the college. Womanhouse was also in a separate space, forty miles away from the school. At Cal Arts, for the first time, I was actually on a full-time day school campus, and as soon as I set foot in it, I began to be uncomfortable. But before I had a chance to really face my discomfort, the school year was over. Lloyd and I went off to Albuquerque, New Mexico, I to make lithographs, he to build sculpture. All through that summer, I kept hoping that things could be patched up between me and Mimi. But she was committed to Cal Arts. I was committed to the development of a female community. I don't know why I didn't realize then that there was a fundamental split between us. I guess that my needs made me hope that our differences could be accommodated. She, however, never acknowledged that our disagreement was philosophical. Rather, she insisted that I was not "grown up" or I would know that one just had to struggle within the structure as it existed and try to change it as best one could. Summer allowed me to get away from that situation that was so terribly painful for me. I didn't want to lose Mimi's "approval," but I wasn't sure that I wanted to commit myself to try to change a male-dominated institution. I was glad that I could plunge into my work and forget about the whole conflict for a while.

All through the spring, I had struggled with my feelings about the split with Mimi in a series of works based upon that grid structure. Her images were closed. The spaces inside my grids opened up. You could see into them; they held a beautiful and peaceful space. But you could not enter those spaces. One's way was barred by a series of flesh beams. It was the human condition that prevented one from re-entering "Childhood." These images led me to another series, one that represented the place I felt myself to be at that moment—moving through the limits of female role. I used the flower as the symbol of femininity, as O'Keeffe had done. But in my images the petals of the flower are parting, and one can see an inviting but undefined space, the space beyond the confines of our own femininity. These works speak of my longing for transcendence and the bitter hopes of all womanhood. They are, in my estimation, my first steps in being able to make clear, abstract images of my feelings as a woman.

In the summer, I made a suite of lithographs on the theme "Through the Flower," and I worked on my book. The book grew and changed as I did. At the end of the summer, Lloyd and I made our first trip to Europe, which affected me deeply by confirming my commitment to my own form language. Seeing the work of the great artists helped me see that their achievement came as much out of their investment in their ideas, whatever those ideas were, as out of their "talent." I came back from our trip refreshed and with a new series of work in my mind. These were to combine my interest in women's history, my identification with women of the past, my knowledge of women's art and literature, and my own imagery. For the past few years, I had immersed myself in looking at women's art.

I had first searched out the work of other women who had made abstract art, looking at it, reading whatever I could about the artists. I examined the work of Barbara Hepworth,

Georgia O'Keeffe, and Lee Bontecou, each of whom worked in a different historic milieu, but who, in my estimation, had something in common with each other and with me. They all seemed to have made a considerable amount of work that was constructed around a center, as I had done. There also seemed to be an implied relationship between their own bodies and that centered image. In my work, I felt a body identification with both the images I made and the surface on which they were painted. I felt myself to be both the image/surface and the artist working on that painting simultaneously. The canvas was like my own skin; I was the painting and the painting was me. Barbara Hepworth said (in A. M. Hammacher's book on her sculpture), "body experience . . . is . . . the center of creation. I rarely draw what I see. I draw what I feel in my body." She suggested that when a male sculptor sees a pregnant woman, he perceives her from the outside, as a form. But Hepworth felt herself to be "the spectator of the object and the object itself." To me, this implies that she felt herself to be both the woman carrying the baby and the sculptor seeing the pregnant woman.

This corresponded with my own experience and I felt that Georgia O'Keeffe made a similar connection between herself and her work. In her paintings, the flower suggests her own femininity, through which the mysteries of life could be revealed. Similarly, Bontecou's stretched canvas forms also seemed to me to possess a body metaphor. They described a mysterious inner space, which is sometimes threatening and sometimes inviting, an embodiment of cultural attitudes toward female sexuality. In my mind, her early work represents her attempt to overthrow social stereotypes about female sexuality by symbolizing them. In much the same way, the

"Pasadena Lifesavers" allowed me to break through my guilt about my emotional range by asking, "Who am I as a woman?" and then symbolizing the various answers.

In 1970, when I became friends with Miriam, she told me of her experiences in San Diego, where she had struggled to make paintings out of *her* feelings as a woman. She also used a central cavity and a spread leg image, as in the painting "OX." When I saw it, I related to it instantly, seeing in its duality of strength and vulnerability, power and receptivity, a parallel to the subject matter of my own paintings. Then, Mimi and I looked at work together, examining paintings and sculptures of women known and unknown, concentrating on those who had worked abstractly. From our experiences as artists, we both had an understanding of how to look for the hidden content in women's work. What we discovered in our studies and later, in our studio visits overwhelmed me; and reinforced my own early perceptions. We found a frequent use of the central image, often a flower, or abstracted flower form, sometimes surrounded by folds or undulations, as in the structure of the vagina. We saw an abundance of sexual forms—breasts, buttocks, female organs. We felt sure that what we were seeing was a reflection of each woman's need to explore her own identity, to assert her sense of her own sexuality, as we had both done. But ". . . the visual symbollogy . . . must not be seen in a simplistic sense as 'vaginal art.' Rather . . . women artists have used the central cavity which defines them as women as the framework for an imagery which allows for the complete reversal of the way in which women are seen in the culture. That is: to be a woman is to be an object of contempt and the vagina, stamp of female-ness, is despised. The woman artist, seeing herself as loathed, takes that very mark of her otherness and by asserting it as the hallmark of her iconography, establishes a vehicle by which to state the truth and beauty of her identity."[1]

It is hard to express the way I felt when I saw the work of so many women artists who had tried, as I had, to deal with their condition as women. Behind the façade of formalized art concerns, these artists had searched out a way to assert their identity through an abstract form language. Mimi and I accumulated a group of slides that focused on work which used a central format as a metaphor for the female self. When we first showed them at the 1971 Rap Weekend in Fresno, women cried and sobbed, throwing themselves into our arms, exclaiming that they had made images like those, that they had been ashamed of them, that their male teachers had sneered at them, that they had thrown them away. This reaction was often repeated whenever the slides were shown and strengthened my belief that my struggle had indeed been a personification of the struggle of many other women artists. The experience of comparing my work to that of other women and of sharing my perception contributed to my belief that, as Barbara Hepworth said, "The woman's approach presents a different emphasis. I think that women will contribute a great deal . . . to the visual arts, and perhaps to sculpture, for there is a whole range of formal perception belonging to the feminine experience. . . ."[2] But how could we make the contribution that Hepworth described if those aspects of our womanhood that *were* expressed in our art were not even acknowledged? I believed that what I and other women artists

[1] Judy Chicago and Miriam Schapiro, "Female Imagery," *Womanspace Journal,* Vol. I, No. 3 (Summer 1973), pp. 11–14.
[2] Herbert Read, *Barbara Hepworth: Carvings and Drawings* (London: Lund, Humphries, 1952).

had done in our struggle to signify ourselves was important, but within the framework of formalist criticism (which was and still is the prevailing critical approach), that importance could never be recognized. Feminist art historian Arlene Raven identified the problem when she said: "When a woman artist positively identifies herself to us through her work, she commits a courageous and daring act of self-exposure, because she expressed herself outside of—and without the support of—a social, economic, and cultural base. She has not participated in the mainstream of the culture, and the culture does not operate from her perspectives. Her contribution has neither spoken to nor been understood by that system, and the content of her art has been bypassed by interpretations which could not reveal it."[3] "Thus, a woman's saying *I am*, I know myself, I understand on the basis of reality how I can act in the world, and I feel a fundamental optimism—a grasp upon my survival as a model for human survival—is saying something which challenges the existing and prevailing world view."[4] This challenge could certainly not affect the society if it were not seen for what it was.

My work and other women's work was always looked at in relation to men's work, never in relation to that of other women. In some ways, this was appropriate, as the women artists who *were* acknowledged in art history had worked within a male milieu. But those women artists whose work I examined, both with Mimi and by myself, functioned in male art communities as I did, yet new aspects of their work and mine appeared when it was juxtaposed against the work of other women artists. Few people seem to have thought of look-

[3] "Woman's Art: The Development of a Theoretical Perspective," *Womanspace Journal,* Vol. I, No. 1 (February/March 1973), pp. 14–20.
[4] Ibid.

ing at women's work next to other women's work to see if the
work's *subject matter,* if not its form, reflected anything of
women's unique experience. In addition to the absence of a
content-oriented criticism, there are larger social reasons for
this. "Women lack concrete means for organizing themselves
into a unit which can stand face to face with the correlative
unit. They have no past, no history. . . . They are not even
promiscuously herded together in the way that creates community feeling. . . . They live dispersed among males, attached through residence, housework, economic condition,
and social standing to certain men . . . more firmly than
they are to other women. . . . The bond that unites her to
her oppressors is not comparable to any other. . . . Here is
to be found the basic trait of woman. She is the Other in a
totality of which the two components are necessary to one
another."[5] It is out of an identification of women with men
rather than with other women that the evaluation of women's
art has taken place. When I started to look at women's art in
terms of common subject matter, I found a series of relationships among the works that strengthened me as an artist. By
identifying the submerged content in other women's work, I
was able to identify my own impulses and the subject matter
those impluses implicitly led me to.

My continuing investigation into women's art brought me
to realize many facts that I had never learned, the first of
which is that there have probably *always* been women artists.
There are cultures in which all the art is and was made by
women. All Navajo blankets are woven by women; almost
all American Indian basketry and pottery was done by women.
"The huts of the Australian, the black camel-hair tents of

[5] Simone de Beauvoir, *The Second Sex* (New York: Alfred A. Knopf,
Inc., 1953), p. xix.

the Bedouin, the yurta of the nomads of Central Asia, the earth lodges of the Omaha, and the pueblos of the Hopi were all the exclusive work of women."[6] Peruvian erotic pottery was the product of female artisans, and Elaine Morgan argues very convincingly in *Descent of Woman* that pottery itself was invented by women.

I was amazed to discover that nuns often worked on medieval manuscript illuminations side by side with monks, but of course no one had ever mentioned that in my class on medieval art. There was even a sculptress, Sabina von Strasbourg in the thirteenth century who worked on the façades of Gothic cathedrals, which implies that all women of the time were not involved in love and romance and chastity belts as social mythology would have it. As I continued my studies, I found out that in different historic periods, women artists functioned and achieved, often in the face of overwhelming difficulties. Some gained honor and recognition in their own time and supported themselves handsomely. Others earned the patronage of various monarchs. In sixteenth-century Italy there was Sofonisba Angussola, Marietta Robusti (Tintoretto's daughter), and Lavinia Fontana. Sofonisba was so well regarded that Anthony Van Dyck left a very moving account of her work. Fontana became one of the most successful portraitists of her day. In Holland, also in the sixteenth century, Catherine von Hemessen, portraitist and miniaturist, had as her patroness the Queen of Hungary.

Despite the fact that I had been taught in school that there were few women artists, I kept discovering more and more. Seventeenth-century Italy produced Artemisia Gentileschi and Rosalba Carriera. Artemisia painted biblical themes;

[6] Nancy Reeves, *Womankind* (Chicago: Aldine-Atherton, Inc., 1971), p. 83.

I found the strength and character of the women in her pictures particularly intriguing and unusual for that historic
period. Carriera did a good number of sumptuous pastels,
one of which I saw and was overwhelmed by in the Louvre.
Judith Leyster was a contemporary of Franz Hals, and I
found a beautiful painting of hers in the Hals Museum in
Holland. Often her work is confused with his, but this might
change if we were able to see an exhibition of her entire
oeuvre. Rachel Ruysch was a highly successful and well-paid
Dutch still-life painter, about whom I was unable to find
much material. Nonetheless, the quality of the paintings I
saw suggests that she has been greatly underrated by history.

In the eighteenth century, Angelica Kauffmann, born in
Switzerland, worked primarily in Italy and was also successful and well-known. In addition to being a court painter, she
painted china for the Meissen factory in Dresden, adapting
her buoyant and delicate images to the surface of porcelain
vases. I loved her work, although I found some of it a bit
sentimental for my taste. In the same period in France, there
were a succession of women artists, like Marguerite Gérard,
the sister-in-law of Fragonard, whose work I saw at the Fragonard Museum. There were some small, lovely etchings of
hers hidden away in a corner of a room. In fact, it seemed
like a great deal of women's work in Europe was at museums
that honored their male contemporaries or relatives, never
them.

In prerevolutionary France, Élisabeth Vigée-Lebrun had
Marie Antoinette as her patroness. Vigée was primarily a
court painter, recording the figures of the nobility. She
was quite successful and competed with Adélaide Labille-
Guiard, not for male attention, but for artistic honors. There
is a whole room in Versailles filled with their work. Both

women worked within the traditional painting modes of their times and both were superb technicians. In the early nineteenth century, Constance-Marie Charpentier was active. Her beautiful painting "Portrait of Charlotte du Val d'Ognes" was, until recently, attributed to David.[7] Shortly after Charpentier, Rosa Bonheur emerged, whose ambition was to surpass the achievements of Vigée-Lebrun. Primarily an animal painter, she had to go to the slaughterhouse and horse fairs in order to study anatomy, because women were excluded from anatomy classes in the academies. In fact, given the number of restrictions against women, it was absolutely amazing to me that so many women managed to achieve distinction, success, and honors.

Even in the early days of America, there were women artists. Sarah and Anna Peale were part of the famous nineteenth-century Peale painting family. Yet their work is hardly ever mentioned when the family is discussed as is the case with the contemporary Wyeth family, which also includes several women artists. Late in the nineteenth century, a number of American expatriated sculptresses settled in Rome, the most famous of whom was Harriet Hosmer, who employed twenty or thirty workmen in her Italian atelier and was the first woman to enter the Rome Academy in sculpture. At the same time, in Germany, Elisabet Ney was battling her way to prominence as the first female to enter the Munich Art Academy in sculpture. These women carved stone and conceived of and executed monumental projects, and still the mythology about women's weakness continued unabated in the culture. Why wasn't there a relationship between the facts of these women's lives and the attitudes toward women

[7] Linda Nochlin, "Why Have There Been No Great Women Artists?," *Art News,* Vol. I, No. 1 (February/March 1973).

and women artists generally? The more I learned, the more upset I became. All these women artists had struggled through the discrimination, the prejudices, the restrictions against women and made themselves visible as artists. In the face of so many obstacles, they carved out lives for themselves in a world where only male artists had the support of the culture.

One day, while we were working in Womanhouse, one of the women in the Feminist Program returned from a thrift-shop expedition carrying an old book. It was an out-of-print edition about something called the Woman's Building, which none of us had ever heard about. Opening the faded, gold-trimmed volume, we excitedly discovered that there had been a building in the 1893 World's Columbian Exposition at Chicago, designed by a woman architect, established and run by a Board of Lady Managers, filled with work by women around the world, including a large mural by "our" Mary Cassatt, as she was referred to by the proud women who organized the building and commissioned her mural. As we examined the book, I was struck by the quality of conscious-ness evidenced by the women involved in the building and by the fact that they had apparently unearthed a good deal of historical material about women artists. The writer of the book referred to many artists from Europe and America with whom I was unfamiliar and also to women artists from Egyp-tian, Cretan, and Greco-Roman times.

Cassatt's mural was a three-part painting entitled "Mod-ern Woman." In it, she portrayed women as independent, self-sufficient, and devoted to learning. The central panel depicted women plucking the fruits of knowledge from trees in an orchard and handing them down to their daughters. On the left, three women pursued the allegorical figure of fame, while on the right, several female figures were involved in the various arts. It was a symbolic painting showing women struggling to move out into the world. Cassatt worked on plans for the mural for a long time; there are a number of studies around. Unfortunately, the mural seems to have been lost sometime after it was removed from the Exhibition, a fitting symbol for our own lost heritage.

Not only did I discover work that related directly to my personal struggle as an artist, but I found out that *many* women before me had broken through female role and made themselves into successful, independent, creative people. Yet the struggles and successes of one generation did not necessarily guarantee greater ease to the women of the next. Instead of the work of one woman attesting to the potential of all women, the work was ripped out of its natural context by male historians. One historical period would allow women more freedom. They would push forward, overcome the restrictions of female role, affirm their talents, realize their abilities. Then male dominance would assert itself again. The women's achievements would be left out of recorded history, and young women could not model themselves upon struggles and accomplishments of their mothers. In each century, women had to try to make a place for themselves without the information that was their natural heritage.

Despite the continuing obstacles, in the late nineteenth and early twentieth centuries, many more women artists emerged. Nearly all of the early art movements of the century had women in them, some of them pivotal figures; yet nearly all of them are ignored in history books. During the Impressionist period in France there was Berthe Morisot, Eva Gonzales, and, of course, Mary Cassatt. Later there was Suzanne Valadon, who worked in almost total secrecy until she was accidentally discovered drawing by Toulouse-Lautrec when he came to her apartment to invite her to a party. She is known almost exclusively as Utrillo's mother and model, although in my opinion her work greatly surpasses his in quality.

Marie Laurencin was a prominent member of the circle around Picasso; Paula Modersohn-Becker was an early Expressionist, whose life was cut short by her death in childbirth at thirty. Gabriele Münter was another woman in the Expressionist movement. Sonia Turk Delaunay appeared on the French art scene with her husband, Robert, and with him invented Orphism, but it is only he who is credited in American art history books. Among the Russian cubists, there were a number of women, most prominently Natalia Goncharova. The Bauhaus in Germany also included a great many women, Sophie Tauber-Arp, Annie Albers, and others. Kay Sage and Merrit Oppenheim were early Surrealists, and there were other independent surrealist women, like Leonor Fini, Leonora Carrington, and Dorothea Tanning. Barbara Hepworth emerged in England in the thirties. Georgia O'Keeffe had already made her appearance in the Stieglitz group in New York. Other women made prominent places for themselves in the world of art, notably Viera de Silva from Portugal, Loren McIver in the United States, Käthe Kollwitz in Germany, and Germaine Richier in France.

The American Abstract Expressionists also had their share of women, like Lee Krasner, Elaine de Kooning, Pearl Fine, and later the second generation: Helen Frankenthaler, Joan Mitchell, Miriam Schapiro, and Grace Hartigan. There were a number of important sculptors working in New York by that time: Louise Nevelson, Louise Bourgeois, Dorothy Dehner. Alice Neel was painting realist paintings in isolation. In the sixties, Nikki de St. Phalle, in Paris; Lee Bontecou,

Marisol, Chryssa, and other women in the United States emerged. Despite the fact of all these established and respected women, the three most widely used art-history surveys still contain between them only one reference to a woman artist.

Until the late nineteenth century, I saw only a few works that could be said to possess any direct reflection of women's experience. Artemisia Gentileschi did a great number of paintings on the theme of "Judith Beheading Holofernes," and she represented this subject in a way that seems to me to be quite distinct from that of her male contemporaries. In men's pictures, Judith is usually depicted as standing passively by while the maid "does the honors" or else the gory deed is not even shown. The men usually painted Judith with slender, reedlike arms which were hardly capable of being lifted to cover a yawn, much less do murder. Artemisia's Judith, however, performs the bloody act herself, hacking off Holofernes' head with arms that are muscular and powerful, arms meant for action, an image of a woman quite different from men's.

I studied women's self-portaits and found that when women painted themselves, they *did* seem to have a vehicle for expressing their own attitude toward themselves as women and artists. Women's self-portraits are ". . . little known, seldom reproduced and never studied as a group . . . (and are) self-affirmations by the artist of her identity as a woman in society . . . the faces of many women artists—as seen by themselves . . . show a strength, self-awareness and depth of personality which make many of the images of women painted by their male contemporaries seem psychologically one-dimensional by contrast. These self-portraits say 'I am' when the images of women painted by men say 'This is what I wish you were'. . . ."[8]

Recently I saw a self-portrait by Judith Leyster in the National Gallery of Art, Washington, D.C., along with one by Rosalba Carriera. Both women painted portraits of themselves as artists, holding brushes or palettes. When I saw the portraits, I was deeply moved. I felt that I was seeing an echo of my identity as an artist across the centuries. Men often painted themselves and each other as artists, but rarely women. In male art, men were always the artist, women the models. But here were *women* saying, "Look, here, I am . . . an artist." The fact that Carriera and Leyster saw themselves differently than male artists saw women was emphasized by the painting that hung beneath the Carriera, painted by a male contemporary. In this painting, a game of cards had just been played. The card table, on the left, had been overturned, as if after a fit of passion by one of the players. In the center was a swooning woman, her bosom heaving, supported by two men who were holding her aloft lest she faint from the effects of just having lost at cards. The stern, strong face of Rosalba Carriera stared out above the fatuous painting below it. Why, oh why, it seemed to ask, has *my* face been hidden away for so long, while this false image of woman has been so publicly displayed?

In the Louvre, I saw a group of drawings and paintings done in the eighteenth century of plans for the Grand Gallery, which was to contain numerous paintings and sculptures and was to be a place where artists could work. Women artists are included almost casually in the plans, sketching, working at easels, side by side with their male counterparts.

8 Paula Harper, from an Unpublished Bibliography, Feminist Art Program, California Institute of the Arts (1972).

In this new edition of Through the Flower, *I decided to include only self-portraits by women artists, rather than the range of work I reproduced in earlier versions of the book. I wanted to emphasize the development of women's consciousness of themselves as creators, which dates back to the Renaissance. In assembling these images, I encountered a rather surprising inconographic void: for example, it took many months and considerable searching to locate a self-portrait by an African-American woman from the nineteenth or early twentieth century. I found this quite odd, considering the number of black women artists who emerged during this period (for example, Elizabeth Catlin, Augusta Savage, Edmonia Lewis, Elizabeth Prophet, and, during the Harlem Renaissance, such women as Laura Willa Waring). Because I had discovered so many self-portraits by European and Anglo-American women artists, I had assumed (wrongly) that it would be relatively easy to locate some by their African-American sisters. Finally, I was aided by the art historians Judith Wilson and Leslie King Hammond. Dr. Hammond explained the striking scarcity of nineteenth-century self-portraits in terms of the specific historic limits on African-American women artists.*

To create a self-portrait, particularly when one represents oneself as an artist, is to assert one's sense of self. Apparently, this was more dangerous for African-American women artists, whose access to artistic support often required public ambiguity about their gender and/or their race. To understand these constraints is to better appreciate the courage required of marginalized and disenfranchised peoples who wished to be artists. To take up a brush, to make a mark, to create a body of work—how valiant the effort, how precious the result.

I believe that it is crucial for women artists to situate ourselves in the context of our own gender, class, and ethnic histories and struggles rather than in relationship to male histories. If we see ourselves only against the background of men's privileges, we are unable to appreciate our own heroic and greatly under-recognized achievements.

I also want to suggest through the continuity of these images that the question that continues to be raised—Why have there been no great women artists?—would be more accurately framed by asking: Why have there been so many great women artists whose work we still do not know?

Years ago I searched the museums of Europe to find scattered examples of women's work. Since then, the National Museum of Women in the Arts has opened in Washington, DC, dedicated to the preservation of our precious cultural heritage. But one institution cannot single-handedly guarantee the equitable inclusion or representation of the glorious array of subject matter, styles, and techniques embodied in women's art. Despite the widespread work done by feminist art historians and critics in the last twenty years, too many young women still graduate from college without adequate knowledge of the rich tradition barely hinted at by these reproductions.

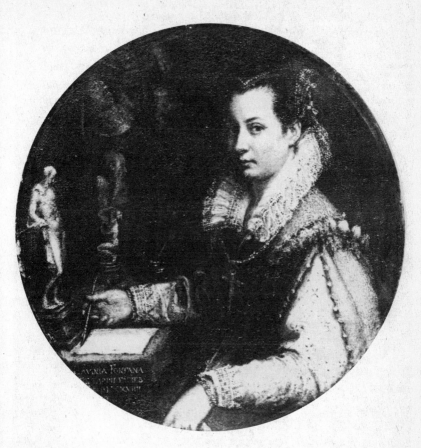

Lavinia Fontana, *Self-Portrait,* 1579 (Photo Uffizi Gallery, Florence, Italy)

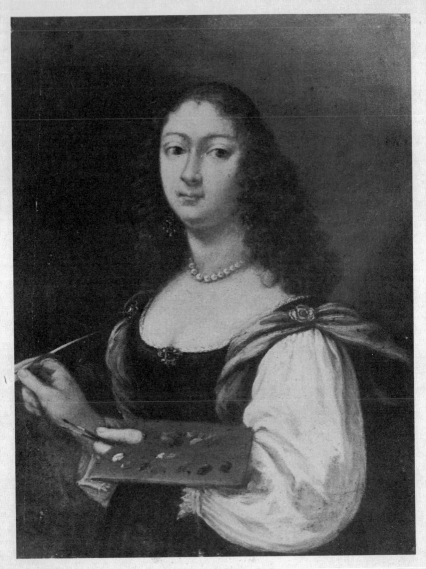

Elisabet Sirani (1638–1665), *Self-Portrait* (Photo Pinacoteca
Nazionale, Bologna, Italy)

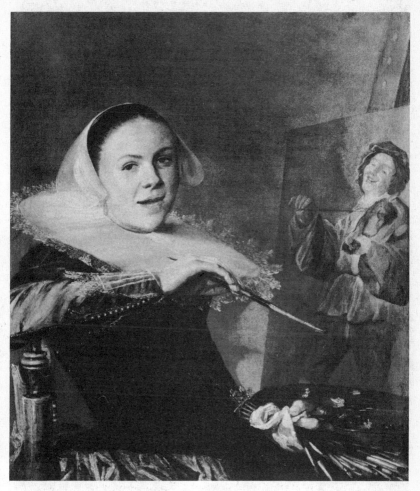

Judith Leyster (1609–1660), *Self-Portrait*, 1635; oil on canvas,
29⅜" x 25⅝" (Gift of Mr. and Mrs. Robert Woods Bliss (1949).
Photo National Gallery of Art, Washington, DC)

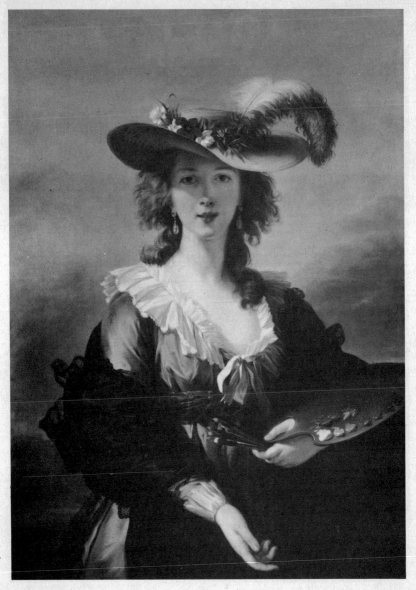

Elizabeth Vigee-Lebrun, *Self-Portrait*, 1782 (Reproduced by courtesy of the Trustees, The National Gallery, London)

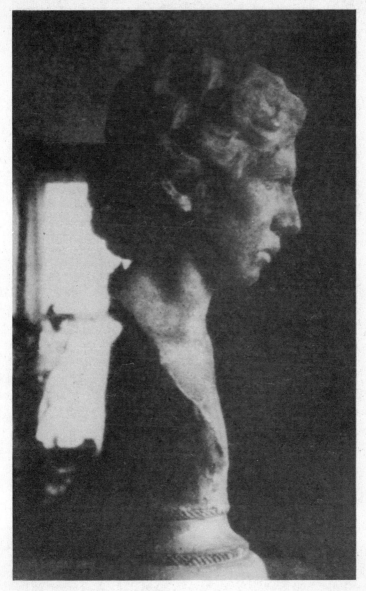

Meta Warrick Fuller, *Self-Portrait* (Photo from *World To-Day* magazine, 1907. Photo Enoch Pratt Free Library, Baltimore, MD)

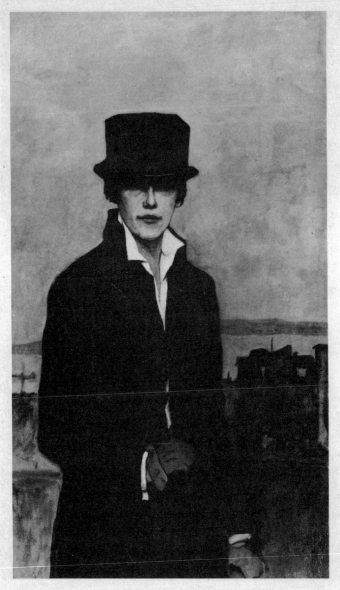

Romaine Brooks, *Self-Portrait*, 1923; oil on canvas, 46¼" x 26⅞" (Photo National Collection of Fine Arts, Smithsonian Institution)

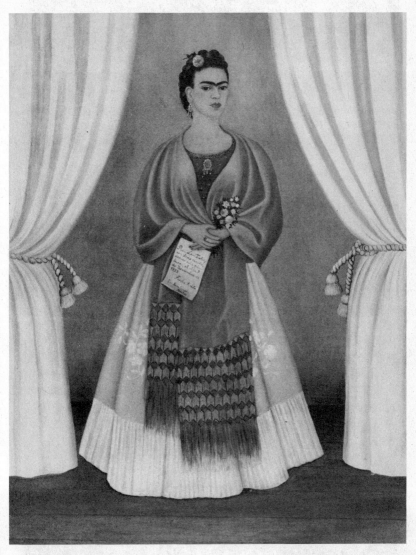

Frida Kahlo, *Self-Portrait Dedicated to Leon Trotsky,* 1937; oil on masonite, 30" x 24" (Gift of the Honorable Clare Booth Luce. Photo National Museum of Women in the Arts, Washington, DC)

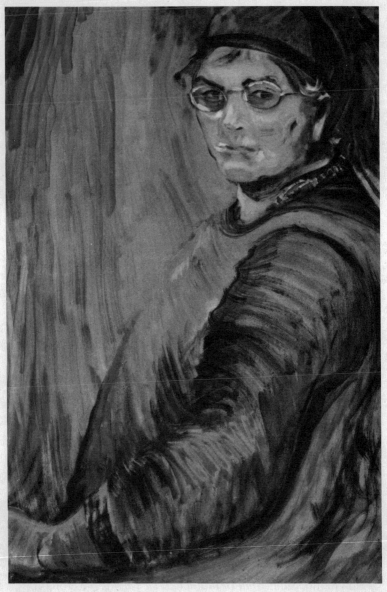

Emily Carr, *Self-Portrait*, 1938–39; oil on paper, 86.36 cm x
58.42 cm (Photo National Gallery of Canada, Ottawa, Canada)

In my historical readings, I discovered that prerevolutionary France seemed to have been relatively accepting of women artists, at least those who were connected with the aristocracy. Then again, their achievements were obscured partly by the French Revolution. But in Europe, revolutionary thought had ushered in a period of concern with "progress" and the "perfectibility" of the human race, including women. The late eighteenth century saw the arrival of Mary Wollstonecraft's *A Vindication of the Rights of Women*. The nineteenth century produced a climate ripe for the birth of feminism in America and later in England. By the midnineteenth century, America was embroiled in struggles over slavery and the rights of women. It seems particularly appropriate that, by the late nineteenth century, inspired by the freedom women were acquiring, an increasing number of American women entered the profession of art, the most significant of whom was Mary Cassatt.

At the Philadelphia Academy, Cassatt had faced the restrictions on art education for women, being unable to work from the nude. She went to Europe, where she established herself as a member of the Impressionist group. Later it was to be alleged by male art history that she was a student of Degas, an untrue assumption based on sexist bias that men are leaders, women followers by definition. In fact, Degas first saw her work in an exhibition and was struck with its excellent draftsmanship. Cassatt immersed herself in the representation of women, children, and their interrelations. In her work, I saw the same sensibility that pervaded women's self-portraits, a perception of women not as sexual creatures, but as real people. Cassatt's women were usually engaged in "doing" something: bathing, caring for or playing with a child, pouring tea, going for a boat ride or a trot in the carriage. Though male artists also dealt with the mother-and-child theme, it was not the exclusive focus of their art, as it was for Cassatt. Her point of view toward her subjects struck me as being remarkably different from that of her male contemporaries. I found myself able to identify with the women in her paintings, whereas I find it difficult to see most paintings of women by men as having anything to do with reality as I experience it.

According to Paula Harper, feminist art historian, many paintings of women by male artists actually represent masculine fantasies about women. Women are presented as idealizations or stereotypes—fleshy, secular nudes, images veiled in religious or mythological significance, maidens, madonnas, sirens, vamps, or witches. Or women are bathed in false purity or religious significance. Classical and baroque art is filled with male fantasies of control and power over women. These are projections by men of their personal erotic fantasies of dominance over women, and they generally associate sexuality with a power/submission relationship. Unfortunately, these works, which reflect and perpetuate masculine attitudes toward women, are too often assumed to be universal images, and few art historians feel the need to point out that these paintings are in fact not universal but, rather, represent the way *one half of the population views the other*.[9]

If men's paintings of women reflect male perception, what do women's paintings about themselves and other women tell us? Examining women's representational work separately from men's made it clear to me that women have not always seen themselves or painted themselves and other women in the same way men have depicted them. In fact, it is possible to see the early self-portraits by women, the work of Cassatt

[9] Ibid.

and her female contemporaries, and increasingly, in the twentieth century, the work of many other women who worked
within a representational format, from the point of view of a
dialogue in which women ask: What is it to be a woman?
The answers are varied. If the self-portraits say: "I am! I, a
woman, *can* be an artist," if Cassatt's women insist that they
are *real* people doing real things, Marie Laurencin's women
explore the nature of female role. Her females are portrayed
as cosmetic creatures, caught in an ambiance of powder and
lipstick. "Her paintings of women with mask-like faces are
often criticized as too pastel and 'sweet' and the subject matter
as trivial and repetitive. But the truth is that prettiness, pastel
sweetness, and claustrophobia are Laurencin's *subject* as well
as her mode. Over and over, she paints women who have no
souls behind their masks; who live in boneless bodies inside
closed rooms."[10]

Käthe Kollwitz, on the other hand, portrays women in
an entirely different manner, not focusing on their imprison-
ment in female role, but rather on their strength. Her women
are powerful and represent the life principle, violently protesting against death and suffering, protecting children and
men alike with their great mothering power. The great Nana
figures of Nikki de St. Phalle present still another aspect of
woman's view of herself. They are robust and playful, neither
threatening nor destructive, but just wonderfully present. Her
large environment "She" is an eighty-five-foot figure of a
woman lying on her back, legs spread. One walks in through
the vagina and explores her entire inner space. "She" is
woman as the source of all life, out of whom we are born,
from whom we receive nourishment and comfort.

[10] Ibid.

Once I began to examine women's work independently from men's, it became obvious that what some women had been trying to say about themselves as women in their art actually *constituted a challenge to male perception* of women and exposed male art as only a *partial,* rather than a universal, perception of reality. The same question about what it means to be a woman that informed the work of many abstract artists was present in women's representational work as well. In subject matter, if not in style, Hepworth and Cassatt, O'Keeffe and Kollwitz, St. Phalle and Bontecou, all confronted a similar dilemma in their development as artists. Their self-images did not correspond to society's definition of women. Asserting their own self-definitions was an implicit step toward challenging the culture and demanding that it adjust its definition of women to correspond to the reality of women's lives, a demand that was not even apprehended, much less met.

Once a woman has challenged the basic values that define her, those that tell her what she is supposed to be as a woman, "She will inevitably challenge others as she discovers in her creative journey that most of what she has been taught to believe about herself is inaccurate and distorted. It is with this differing self-perception that the woman artist moves into the world and begins to define all aspects of experience through her own modes of perception, which, at their very base, differ from the society's."[11]

My investigation of women's art led me to the conclusion that much of the work of women (and, in my estimation, the best and most revolutionary work) possesses a world view, a set of values, and a perception of reality that differs funda-

[11] Judy Chicago and Miriam Schapiro, "Female Imagery," *Womanspace Journal,* Vol. I, No. 3 (Summer 1973), pp. 11–14.

mentally from the dominant perspective of our culture. In order to perceive and appreciate this work, it must be approached with the understanding that men's view of women is just the tip of a gigantic iceberg. Men's refusal to accept woman's view of herself as expressed in her art actually reflects men's larger denial of reality—human vulnerability, weakness, and mortality.

By excluding the work of women artists from history, men not only maintain control of women, but also of the world. We are allowed to identify ourselves and our relationship to the world only through men's perception of reality. Since men assume that their view of reality is the "real" one, they measure our perceptions against theirs and, because they *are* dominant, validate our point of view only to the degree that it corresponds with their own. The silence about women in history, about women's accomplishments, and most importantly, about women's point of view as it is expressed in art, is not an accident of history. Each woman's work, seen only in juxtaposition with men's work, has been rendered impotent by being separated from the work of other women. Seen together, women's work can challenge our most fundamental ideas about women, men, our roles, our potential, our identities, and our priorities.

Investigating women's art helped me see my circumstances and frustration as an artist as a social and political dilemma that could only be solved by a fundamental change in the nature of society. Being denied the recognition I deserved, being rejected by the male art community, and having my achievements and point of view as an artist denied and diminished were all symptoms of my situation as a woman in a male-dominated culture.

8

Learning from the Past

I turned to women's literature in an effort to see if the same point of view I was discovering in art might also be present in women's writings. Previously, I had read women's books randomly, picking out books by women authors whose names I had heard mentioned. If I liked a book, I continued reading work by that woman until I had exhausted her output. In this way, I managed to read quite a few works by contemporary women novelists. But when I went to Fresno, I decided to read systematically. I wanted to see not only if a female point of view was present in any of the work, but if there was any relationship between writers, whether there was a historical development of ideas, and what the social context was that had produced the writer. I chose the work of twelve women who were major writers and whose work spanned two hundred years and three countries. I chose for my study Jane Austen, Charlotte Brontë, George Eliot, George Sand, Edith Wharton, Colette, Gertrude Stein, Virginia Woolf, Willa Cather, Simone de Beauvoir, Anaïs Nin, and Doris

Lessing. I had to abandon my plan to examine George Sand's work, because I could not find enough of her books in translation or in print, despite the fact that she had written 120 books and was a major political and literary force in her own time.

I read these works in search of information that could be relevant to my own life and approached women's literature as I did women's art—*in terms of content*. Did these women concern themselves with their lives and feelings as women? If so, what did they have to say about that subject? Did their work reflect their own struggles as women? I knew that any woman of accomplishment must have faced discrimination as a woman. How had she solved it? What record had she left that could help me? Was there any development in ideas that could be traced in their work?

The first thing that I learned was that women writers, like women artists, worked within the prevailing aesthetic modes of their times. Apparently, until recently, there were simply no other options. They were generally dealt with critically in relation to the concerns of contemporary male writers. Because I approached their work in terms of their lives as women, I found that, although the work *did* relate to that of male writers, there was also a dimension that was singular. This had to do with the fact that most of the women had addressed themselves to the issue of women's condition and had dealt with it in a way that reflected their personal identification with that condition.

In almost all the work I studied, the writers cried out against the pain they had seen women suffer and had suffered themselves. Jane Austen described the limited lives of the women of her time, who were dominated and circumscribed by men. George Eliot's heroines twisted and squirmed under the restrictions imposed upon them because of their sex; Charlotte Brontë's female characters struggled against the confines of their lives and fought for independence. In Edith Wharton's work, women are crushed by male dominance. Lily Bart in *House of Mirth* is seen as being totally victimized by the role she is forced to play. Colette depicted the cloistered arena in which women spend their lives and energy— the world of love, the private world, which is overly perfumed and suffocating like a Marie Laurencin painting. In Colette's novels, the bedroom is often the boundary of female life and the only escape left to Léa, the heroine of the novel *Chéri,* is old age and its consequent sexlessness.

Anaïs Nin recorded the slow emergence from female role, the flights into fantasy, the struggle to take herself seriously, the symbolic battle with the father. Simone de Beauvoir avoided confronting her life as a woman until she was forty, but then she could no longer ignore it. She faced her condition as a woman, examined it in terms of history, and was able to distance herself from the pain. But she understood what can happen to the psyche of the female in male society, and she recorded her knowledge in the book *Woman Destroyed*. But again, as always, she became better known for her novel about her male contemporaries, *The Mandarins.* In the same way, when Anaïs' *Diaries* were first published, the publishing house thought their significance lay in their record of the struggles of "important male authors" like Henry Miller. They were shocked to discover that the developing female audience cared more about Anaïs' struggles than Henry's.

Willa Cather's books document the heroic lives of pioneer women and farm women, who loom much larger than the more frightened, timid men. Doris Lessing followed the struggle for liberation in her character Martha Quest. Her book *The Golden Notebook* is a sensitive and important study of the conflicts of a liberated woman in the sixties. Virginia Woolf wrote both essays and novels which reflected her great concern for women, her understanding of women's circumstances, and her belief in not only the existence, but the worth of a female point of view. Of all the women whose work I studied, only Gertrude Stein did not openly concern herself with women's situation. Yet, although she rarely dealt directly with the subject matter of women's oppression, the nature of her writing reveals an attitude quite different from that of her male contemporaries. Virginia Woolf, who first articulated the idea of a female sensibility in literature thought that the initial step in forging such a sensibility would be the remaking of the sentence, an interesting notion in relation to Stein's work.

I would say that, directly or indirectly, the struggle that these women faced as women was reflected in the books they wrote. However, to learn more about their personal struggles, I began to read biographies, first theirs, then all I could get my hands on. I discovered that almost every woman in history who accomplished anything did so in the face of great prejudice, rejection, and discrimination. The biographies of these women told the same story again and again: a woman of genius, of talent, of aspiration, of intelligence, forced, like Eliot or Brontë, to publish under men's names, or like Austen, to hide their work. Eliot, in fact, edited a magazine which, for a long time, she could not publish in. Colette, whose early work was published under her husband's name, had to sue him for title to her own work.

After reading biographies, I began to study women's political and social history in an effort to understand the social context in which the women had written. It was then that I made the discovery that women's writing and women's art had actually developed against the background of two hundred years of women's struggle for freedom. The twelve women whose work I studied did not emerge singly, as popular mythology would have it (the "if you're really good, you'll make it" story). Rather, they wrote either during or after a period of active feminist struggle, or if spirited political battles were not actually taking place, they generally had the support of a small group of women or were sustained by the companionship of one woman, as were Rosa Bonheur, Willa Cather, and Gertrude Stein.

Jane Austen, whom Virginia Woolf described as the first significant female writer, appeared shortly after the publication of Mary Wollstonecraft's radical book *A Vindication of the Rights of Women*. At that time, there was also, in England, a group of "blue stockings," not the least of whom were the "Sisters of Llangollen." These two spinsters established a life style that women made pilgrimages to observe, one set up as an alernative to the slavery that marriage was for most women then. Moreover, Jane Austen was certainly not the sole woman working then; there were a number of women authors making a living from their work.

Beginning about the 1830s, women had started to openly contend for political rights. For the next half century, they challenged more and more of the restrictions men had placed upon them. It was during this time that Eliot, Brontë, and Sand wrote, and all three of them reflected the growing consciousness spawned by the feminist revolution. As the revolution continued, more and more women writers and artists emerged. Virginia Woolf herself wrote against the atmosphere of a violent fight for women's rights in England. While the female activists were battling the society to a standstill and obtaining the right to hold property, to speak publicly, to divorce, to receive higher education, to enter more of the professions, to control their own earnings, to practice contraception, to have some authority in relation to their children, and, finally, to vote, women writers were articulating the feelings of women caught between old values and new aspirations.

Often, political writers and novelists articulated the same ideas. Sarah Grimke, the abolitionist and feminist, argued in 1840 that "the most perfect social system can only be attained where the laws which govern the sexes are based on justice and equality."[1] While the Grimke sisters were challenging society's rule that women could not speak publicly, and were standing up to the condemnation of the Church, Charlotte Brontë, in England, was wrestling with the question of a woman's fundamental duty. Must she accommodate herself to social mores, Brontë mused, through the character of Jane Eyre, or was her first duty to her own values, even if those values were in conflict with the society's? Alone and poverty-stricken, she stumbled out of Mr. Rochester's house to make her way in the world, having concluded that any sort of deprivation was better than violating her beliefs. Only when Rochester is humbled by his circumstances and can meet her on the basis of their mutual need does Jane consent to be his wife. She reached the same conclusion as had Sarah Grimke: Only through mutuality could a social system exist that allowed men and women equal justice.

At a time when women were confined in limiting and unhealthy clothing, both Brontë and Sarah Grimke expressed their anger that women were made into sex objects through

[1] Gerda Lerner, *The Grimke Sisters* (New York: Schocken Books, 1971), p. 316.

clothes and finery. Brontë, in 1847, wrote in *Jane Eyre:*
"Glad was I to get him out of the silk warehouse and then
out of a jeweller's shop; the more he bought me, the more my
cheek burned with a sense of annoyance and degradation.
. . . I never can bear being dressed like a doll by Mr.
Rochester, or sitting like a second Danae . . . with the golden
shower falling daily round me. . . . He smiled and I thought
his smile was such as a sultan might, in a blissful and fond
moment, bestow on a slave his gold and gems had enriched.
. . . It would, indeed, be a relief, I thought, if I had ever so
small an independency."[2] (In *A Room of One's Own,* published eighty years later, Virginia Woolf argued that Brontë's
notion of a "small independence" was indeed the first step to
personal freedom.)

In 1837, Sarah Grimke had written: "He has adorned the
creature, whom God gave him as a companion, offered in-
cense to her vanity, and made her the instrument of his selfish
gratification, a plaything to please his eye. . . ."[3] Did Brontë
read Grimke's words, or were women around the world simultaneously feeling the same necessity to protest against their
circumstances?

While the Grimkes were striving for women's rights in
America, while Harriet Hosmer was entering the Art Academy in Rome, while Elisabet Ney was struggling to be admitted to the Academy in Munich, while George Eliot was
trying to place her writing in the magazine she edited, Elizabeth Barrett Browning was pleading for the rights of the female creator in her epic poem *Aurora Leigh.* Aurora's cousin
Romney says to her: "Women as you are, mere women, per-

[2] New York: Pocket Books, Inc., 1953, p. 303.
[3] *Up from the Pedestal,* ed. Eileen S. Kraditon, from Sarah Grimke's
Pastoral Letter (Chicago: Quadrangle Books, 1970), p. 55.

sonal and passionate, you give us doting mothers, and perfect
wives, Sublime Madonnas and enduring saints: We get no
Christ from you—and verily We shall not get a poet, in my
mind." Aurora's angry reply is a statement as relevant now as
then: "For me, perhaps I am not worthy, as you say. Of work
like this; perhaps a woman's soul Aspires, and not creates;
yet we aspire. And yet I'll try out your perhapses, sir, And if
I fail . . . why burn me up my straw like other false works.
. . . I'll not ask for grace. . . . I who love my art, would
never wish it lower To suit my stature. I may love my art.
You'll grant that even a woman may love art. *Seeing that to
waste true love on anything is womanly, past question*"[4]
(emphasis mine). Aurora, like Jane Eyre, refuses Romney's
offer for marriage, a brave act in the midnineteenth century,
when women had few means of supporting themselves if they
chose not to be dependent upon men. Yet woman after
woman was standing up to the society and refusing to submit to the subjugation of the female sex.

As Elizabeth Barrett Browning was pleading for Aurora's
right to be a poet, Elizabeth Cady Stanton, in America, was
arguing that women's clothing cramped her in the same way
that she was cramped by female role: "I hazard nothing in
saying that the dress and degradation of an American woman
is as vital as that between the cramped foot and degradation
of a Chinese woman."[5] Later, Eliot used that same metaphor
in Mme. Deronda's statement about the compression of female personality. When Mme. Deronda speaks about her anguish as a creative woman, she compares her situation to that

[4] Elizabeth Barrett Browning, *Aurora Leigh* (London: Smit, Elder &
Co.), pp. 51–61.
[5] Elizabeth Cady Stanton, "Correspondence Between Gerrit Smith and
E. C. Stanton," *Up from the Pedestal* (Chicago: Quadrangle Books,
1970), p. 127.

of a Chinese woman whose feet are bound. When she talked
about having a man's force of genius in a woman's body, she
echoed Margaret Fuller's words, written forty years before:
" 'Tis an evil lot to have a man's ambition and a woman's
heart."[6]

Not only were women novelists and political activists expressing similar ideas, but one woman's work often directly
inspired another's. Mary Wollstonecraft's book, in addition
to contributing to a permissive atmosphere for female writers,
altered the lives of many young women, among whom was
Mary Lamb. After Wollstonecraft's death, Mary Lamb often
visited her husband, William Godwin, who was a publisher.
Mary Lamb was the sister of Charles Lamb, the honored
English essayist, many of whose books she coauthored, although only he received credit. She certainly read the Wollstonecraft book, and in 1813 published "Essay of Needle-
work." This short piece took Wollstonecraft's ideas and extended them into the area of political economy. She argued
that women's work in the home should be paid, a principle
that two hundred years of effort has not yet implemented.

In America, a man named Timothy Fuller read Wollstonecraft's book and decided to educate his daughter, Margaret.
She later wrote the first feminist document in this country,
Woman in the Nineteenth Century. She also set up a series of
conversations for women. She felt that, as women were then
still deprived of higher education, the best method of inform-
ing them was through dialogue. These discussions, aimed at
educating the women of Boston, were attended by a number
of women later active in the feminist movement, including
Elizabeth Cady Stanton. Fuller herself was influenced by both

[6] Faith Chipperfield, *In Quest of Love* (New York: Coward-McCann,
Inc., 1957), Frontispiece.

Mme. de Staël and George Sand. Another woman, Harriet Beecher Stowe, read and was inspired by De Staël, Sand, and Fuller, as well as Harriet Martineau, an Englishwoman who wrote on religion, political economy, property, taxes, labor, and who, in 1837, advocated suffrage for women. Stowe's book *Uncle Tom's Cabin* had such an effect on her generation that when Lincoln met her, shortly after the start of the Civil War, he took her hand in his and said: "So, this is the little lady who made this big war."[7] And, of course, it was the abolition movement that was the stepping-stone to the feminist revolution at the end of the nineteenth century.

Some of these women even managed to make contact with each other. When Margaret Fuller went to Europe, she visited George Sand. Fuller was announced by the maid. Sand did not at first recognize the name. When Sand came downstairs, she realized that this was the woman who had written *Woman in the Nineteenth Century.* Sand threw her arms around her and cried, "My sister." Then the two women went into the study and closed the door. They did not emerge for twenty-four hours. On the same trip, Fuller saw Elizabeth Barrett Browning in Rome. Other frequent visitors at the Browning home were the French painter Rosa Bonheur and Harriet Hosmer, the expatriated American sculptor. Later, on Susan B. Anthony's trip to England, she met a young woman named Emmeline Pankhurst, who adapted Anthony's methods to the suffrage struggle in England. Anthony herself is said to have turned to Hosmer's sculptures for comfort and support whenever she became depressed.

The accomplishments of the nineteenth-century women were staggering. In America, women crisscrossed the country,

[7] Johanna Johnston, *Runaway to Heaven*—A Biography of Harriet Beecher Stowe (New York: Doubleday & Co., 1963), p. 357.

lecturing, entreating, gathering petitions, collecting nickels, dimes, and quarters to establish colleges for women. Susan B. Anthony had so much impact upon the society that in the 1893 World's Columbian Exposition at Chicago, thousands of people cheered her whenever she appeared. In fact, the Woman's Building at the Exposition would not have existed if it had not been for her. The Exposition, as originally planned, did not include any representation of women. Anthony, outraged, went to Washington and gathered together the signatures of the wives of the most influential men of the city. She presented this to Congress, which, in response, established the Board of Lady Managers. Then Anthony remained in the background, as she was anxious lest her radicalism frighten off support for the Woman's Building, which the Board had established. Not only was women's work from around the world exhibited there, but there was a World Congress of Women held at the building, a congress whose impact was felt in the numerous countries represented by the women who attended it.

There were great women's crusades in the last half of the nineteenth century. There were not only the feminist movement, but also the temperance movement, the missionary movement, and the women's club movement, which Charlotte Perkins Gilman, an active feminist speaker and writer, called "one of the most important sociological phenomena of the century—indeed of all centuries, marking . . . the first timid steps toward social organization of these so long unsocialized members of our race. Now the whole country is budding into women's clubs. The clubs are uniting and federating by towns, states, nations; there are even world organizations. The sense of human unity is growing daily among women."[8]

[8] Page Smith, *Daughters of the Promised Land* (Boston: Little, Brown and Company, 1970), pp. 265–66.

Women were organizing, writing, speaking, painting, sculpturing, and were pushing into *all* the professions. Elizabeth Blackwell became the first female physician in America. Earlier, Victoria Woodhull and her sister had become the first female stockbrokers; then, later, Woodhull became the first woman to run for the presidency. In England, Florence Nightingale was beginning her lonely battle to establish nursing as a profession, not only training women, but establishing schools and methodology. Everywhere, women were being born who would challenge male culture and male assumptions about "woman's place," and women writers were articulating those challenges.

In Poland, in 1867, Marja Skodovska was born, who, as Marie Curie, discovered radium. In Russia, Emma Goldman made her appearance in 1869, later to shake American society with her radical ideas about women's rights, anarchism, and social change. The sociologist Jane Addams, born earlier, in 1860, made important contributions in the field of social work and was one of the most popular and influential women of her time. In 1879, Margaret Sanger was born. Almost single-handedly she introduced contraception methods into this country, protesting all the laws against the dispensing of birth-control information. There was almost no aspect of the culture that was left untouched by the efforts of women. There was indeed a great awakening of womanhood taking place. Kate Chopin's book appropriately titled *The Awakening* speaks poignantly of the new sense of freedom women were experiencing: ". . . when she was there beside the sea, absolutely alone, she cast the unpleasant, pricking garments from her, and for the first time in her life stood naked in the open air, at the mercy of the sun, the breeze that beat upon her, and the waves that invited her. How strange and awful it seemed to stand under the sky! How delicious! She felt like some newborn creature, opening its eyes in a familiar world that it had never known."[9]

I read this book after I had been studying women's work and history for several years, and was profoundly moved by it. How different it appeared to me than it might have, had I not seen it against the context of women's social, political, and aesthetic challenge to male culture! I thought about my experiences in school. I had read work by nineteenth-century women writers, but because that work had never been discussed in relation to the "awakening" of female consciousness, my appreciation of it had been greatly diminished. By the time I was in college, in the fifties and early sixties, there was almost no mention of the political activity of women in the nineteenth century; the feminist revolution had become only a footnote. The great wave of feminism had subsided after the suffrage movement, and then it had been obscured by history.

There is a great deal of speculation among modern-day feminists as to the reason for the decline of the feminist revolution and its subsequent absence from history. I myself feel that, even after the laws were changed through political agitation, the values and attitudes that shaped women's personalities and behavior remained the same. Even though the nineteenth-century women changed many of the legal restrictions against women and forced open many of the professions, they were still expected to conform to the concept of what a woman was. Thus "female role" continued to dictate women's lives even when there were no longer many legal reasons why women could not participate fully in the society. Though the nineteenth century left us with new freedoms, it

[9] Kate Chopin, *The Awakening* (New York: Avon Books, 1972), p. 189.

also left us with personalities shaped by male-dominated society. Women still suffered from feelings of inferiority and
helplessness, and the culture reinforced those feelings by elim-
inating the history of the great feminist revolution.

This meant that women born in the mid-twentieth century
were deprived not only of an understanding of their political
and social history, but also of the information about women's
lives contained in women's books and the new definitions of
women asserted in women's art. The fact that women's work
was not viewed as a coherent body of information rendered it
powerless to transmit the new values it contained and left us
with the legacy of freedom the nineteenth-century feminists
provided, but without the necessary redefinitions of self that
real growth demands.

Moreover, even though women made inroads into the professions, they did not have sufficient control over the mechanisms of those professions—the recording of history, the dis-
seminating of information, the transmitting of new values.
Although women had changed the face of society, they did
not have the power to enforce that change, particularly since
they had not yet been able to directly face the issue of the
definitions of "masculine" and "feminine." Virginia Woolf
argued that the feminist challenge of the nineteenth and early
twentieth centuries met with a mounting reaction from men
as that challenge began to affect the concept of masculinity
and all the privilege and power that that concept denotes.
It became clear that both women's art and women's literature
reflected that challenge implicitly and explicitly.

Women writers' descriptions of women's real circumstances
and feelings, their depictions of men (which are often criticized by male critics as being "unrealistic"), women artists'
portrayals of women as real people and their abstract images

of self-awareness and self-assertion, all can be seen as part of women's attempt to change not only women's political and social status, but the very notions we have of masculinity and femininity. The following statement by Woolf illuminates one of the primary issues involved in both the understanding and valuation of women's point of view in art and literature. ". . . the fathers were met, as the nineteenth century drew on, by a force which had become so strong in its turn that it is much to be hoped that psychologists will find some name for it. The old names as we have seen are futile and false. 'Feminism' we have had to destroy. 'The emancipation of women' is equally inexpressive and corrupt. . . . Moreover, none of these tags and labels express the real emotions that inspired the daughters' opposition to the infantile fixation of the fathers. . . ." (Here, Woolf uses the term "infantile fixation" to denote men's need to dominate women.) "Tears were behind it, of course, bitter tears. . . . All we can safely say about that force was that it was a force of tremendous power. It forced open the doors of the private house. It opened Bond Street and Piccadilly; it opened cricket grounds and football grounds; it shrivelled flounces and stays. . . . But it was not the end, it was the beginning. . . . For it was connected with manhood itself. . . . It was those motives, those rights and conceptions that were now challenged. . . ."[10]

The response of male culture was to deny that the challenge had ever taken place, just as male culture still denies the implicit challenge of women's art. Virginia Woolf was right: the very notion of manhood was indeed being challenged, albeit indirectly. The thrust behind the nineteenth century

[10] Virginia Woolf, *Three Guineas* (New York: Harcourt, Brace, & World, Inc., 1938).

feminist revolution manifested itself in women's attempt to describe women's real conditions and feelings in literature and to assert a new image of women in art. The redefinition of the female is the first step in the act of changing the society, its values, and its priorities, and it is no mere coincidence that the present women's movement is based upon the examination and alteration of female role through consciousness-raising.

However, men's desire to maintain their dominance, their suppression of women's history, and their resistance to perceiving the world through women's eyes are not the only explanations for the fact that women's world view has remained submerged. Again according to Woolf, "the subjugation of women . . . was . . . both cause and symptom of a fundamental imbalance in society.[11] According to her, "lack of wholeness in the modern world . . . could only be changed through the introduction of a feminine sensibility."[12] She then went on to argue that . . . "the writing of women, when they discovered their own mode of expression would differ essentially from that of men."[13]

Studying women's art and literature made it clear that most female creators had *not* had a mode of expression that was essentially different from men's. Rather, they, as I, had embedded a different *content,* in the prevailing aesthetic mode of their time, and in so doing, had rendered their point of view invisible to mainstream culture. Only in the twentieth century was there any attempt to express the idea that the *form of art itself* would have to be different if it was to communicate a female point of view.

Woolf maintained that the articulation of female experi-

[11] Herbert Marder, *Feminism and Art* (Chicago: University of Chicago Press, 1968), p. 30.
[12] Ibid.
[13] Ibid., p. 21.

ence could bring about a softening of the eternal conflict between opposites corresponding, roughly speaking, to masculine and feminine principles. But this was only possible if
women found a way to make "a language that weds idea to
feeling."[14] She believed that women had to find a "new
style appropriate to new subject matter" that could lead to
the opening of hitherto obscure regions of women's minds."[15]
Anaïs Nin put it another way.

Writing in her second *Diary,* she articulated her desire to
create . . . "Without those proud delusions of man, without
megalomania, without schizophrenia, without madness. . . ."
Rather, she wanted her art to ". . . be the closest to the life
flow. I must install myself inside of the seed, growth, mysteries
. . . art must be like a miracle. Before it goes through the
conduits of the brain and becomes an abstraction, a fiction,
a lie. It must be for women, more like a personified ancient
ritual, where every spiritual thought was made visible, en-
acted, represented."

In examining the work of Woolf and Nin, I had discovered
a quality of transparency, both in the writing and in the
imagery. I asked Anaïs about it and she spoke about the
"transparency of the psyche"—the sense of being able to see
through successive layers to the very core of reality. I really
identified with that, I had always been able to "read" art (i.e.,
identify its "content"). I knew, through my study of women's
work, that it was primarily the *content* that differentiated
women's work from men's when there was a difference. This
realization helped me affirm one of my own impulses as an
artist—to make my work openly subject-matter oriented
(while still being abstract) and to try to reveal intimate
emotional material through my forms.

[14] Ibid.
[15] Ibid.

That quality of transparency also made me think of Georgia O'Keeffe's paintings. It is interesting that she is actually a contemporary of Nin's. But, because of the decline of feminism and the obscuring of its history, all three women were left without a context but with the fruit of feminist consciousness. Each functioned in almost total isolation and each endured her own torture. I felt that I entirely understood why Woolf committed suicide: one day she just could no longer muster the energy to fight the structure of male-dominated society; why O'Keeffe went to New Mexico to live alone: it was probably the only way she could live without the constant impingement of male values and perceptions; why Nin wrote secretly in her *Diaries* and suffered terrible anguish when they were going to be published: she had lived so long without having her experience affirmed that she herself had come to fear that it might "all be a dream."

Before the women's movement, I felt that I, too, was faced with those same three choices: commit suicide, work in isolation, or accept the absence of recognition. Each one of these women had to live her life and do her work *without the affirmation of the society*. I know that both Woolf and Nin turned to the work of other women for support, affirmation, and help. O'Keeffe is the only one of the three who resisted articulating her commitment to a female art, despite the fact that her work clearly reflects that commitment. But, although she refused to allow her work to be reproduced in my book, the facts of her life and the strength of her images speak louder than do her fears of standing with other women. The work of Woolf, Nin, and O'Keeffe, combined with my new knowledge of women's art, literature, and history, provided me with the impetus, the confidence, the nourishment, and the ideas to enrich my own form language so that it could allow me to truly be myself as a woman artist.

9

Getting It Together

I had discovered my heritage as a woman. However, my knowledge existed in somewhat of a vacuum, as the society certainly does not reflect the fact of women's achievements, women's perceptions, and all of the work women have made. I recognized that my work could only be accurately understood against the background of female history, and I wanted to find a way to incorporate that history into my work so that the viewer would be forced to confront my work in the context of other women's work. I decided to do a series of paintings entitled "The Great Ladies," which I began in 1972 and completed at the end of 1973. At first, they were purely visual images, named after various women in history who transcended female role through the fact that they were rulers or women of great achievement. After a while, I felt that I wanted to make the paintings more specific and to insist that the content of the painting be observed. I did this by using words in conjunction with the images that described the lives of the women and why I identified with them.

Then I began to write other things on the paintings—personal experiences, comments about books I was reading. I wanted to demystify the art process and make it accessible to others. Several of my friends commented about these works, telling me that they felt very moved by them. I realized that I had stumbled on the means of wedding my feminism and my art. When I made abstract images of my feelings, many people did not know how to "read" those images. By writing about the idea I was working with visually, perhaps the viewer would then be able to recognize the meaning of the image. That way, I would be educating people to understand my work while they were looking at it. This was a big step in making my content clear and comprehensible without having to deny my own artmaking process.

Anaïs' comments about the quality of transparency in women's work had helped me identify and validate one of my own impulses. My ability to see "through form" and recognize content had always embarrassed me because I could "read" not only art content, but also the meaning of human behavior. Seeing "the transparency of the psyche" in other women's work, relating to it, liking it, helped me accept that this ability was part of my gift as a woman. I decided to "expose" my perceptions by writing them down on my paintings— writing whatever I was feeling while I was making the work, so that my process and my image became "transparent" and understandable to others.

My readings, my studies of women's art, and the developing female art community were combining to make me feel more comfortable about myself, to feel confident about exposing my real feelings, and to relax and feel less anxious about myself. I was also emerging from seeing myself through the limiting stereotypes available to women in male culture. In my efforts to avoid being considered a "dumb cunt," I had accepted being seen in terms of another stereotype, that of the "superwoman." To protect myself, I had learned to hide my needs and to get what I needed through giving to others. In the context of the growing female community, I was experiencing myself in a new way. Some women perceived me as men did: strong, invulnerable, defensive, manipulative. But there were others who were able to see me as I really was: strong but vulnerable, powerful but accessible, strong-minded but open. As I saw my own perceptions of myself reflected in their views of me, I was able to expose more and more of my softness, my shyness, my fears, and my needs. This process had a profound effect on my work.

I had always set up a rigid working schedule, working out all the paintings in advance, and then executing them. The opening up of my personality resulted in an opening up of my work process. I planned a series of works, including "The Great Ladies," but I changed my plans as I went along, allowing myself to respond to my needs of the moment. In addition to "The Great Ladies" paintings, I made a series of other works in which I used the air brush more intuitively. First I set up a system and masked and sprayed. But then, after the system was established, I began to modify it, to change it, to work directly on the surface of the painting without a plan, pushing the painting to see how far it would go. I no longer had to hide my content inside the structure. I had a new audience for my work.

The first time I really absorbed the fact of this new audience was after Womanspace had opened in January 1973. I was on the Exhibition Committee, and we decided to do an exhibition of women who had worked abstractly and dealt with issues about sexuality. There was a lot of discussion around the country then about "central core imagery," and the Exhibition Committee had decided to do the first show about female sexuality. We had a good many intense discussions and examined a lot of work. At a certain point in the discussion, I realized that these women really understood the issues I had been trying to articulate in "Pasadena Life-savers." I decided to make a painting that dealt with the same subject matter I had dealt with in 1969, but I wanted to make the content more overt, to reflect the new permission available because of the women's movement. When I went into my studio, I realized that I was painting this painting for a *female audience*. I was not thinking about the galleries or the museum or the male artists. I only thought about the women on the Exhibition Committee—and I knew that they would understand the painting. For the first time in my life, I knew that my audience would connect with my art.

I want to point out that I was not painting this picture for anyone but myself. Rather, it is common for artists to visualize their work in the environment in which it will be hung. Moreover, the nature of the "issues" of the art community dictates a great deal of the art that is done in that community. Once I felt that the women of the exhibition committee would relate to my work, I no longer cared if the art community itself related to it. I had found another context, another audience, another environment for my work. This was a crucial moment in my development as an artist because I was thinking about *what women would think about my work*. This liberated me and made me able to express aspects of myself that I couldn't deal with as long as I was thinking about male response.

When I finished "Let It All Hang Out," the name of the picture for the sexuality show, I cried for several hours. The painting was forceful and yet feminine. I had never seen those two attributes wedded together in an image. I felt ashamed—like there was something wrong with being feminine and powerful simultaneously. Yet I felt relieved to have finally expressed my power. I could never have shown it comfortably if it were not for the growing support of the female art community.

The fact of this support forced me into a conflict. The Feminist Art Program was supported by a male-dominated school. I was committed to building a female community. I was drawing my sustenance as an artist increasingly from that community. The values of the female community and the Fresno Program as I had developed it were basically opposed to the values of Cal Arts, which was hierarchical in structure and directed exclusively toward the small, elitist art community. When the Fresno Program came into Cal Arts as the Feminist Art Program, I was very excited about the fact that an art school was addressing itself specifically to the needs of the female students. But after we began working on the campus, I became aware that something was going wrong in the program.

I had tried, within the program, to help my students realize themselves through their lives and feelings as women—to be themselves, even if that meant revealing their primitivism— and to express themselves honestly. This is what I was also trying to do in my art, and by the end of 1972, I was able to derive support from the female art community for doing so. But the Feminist Art Program was forty miles away from Womanspace and isolated within a male-dominated school. We had private quarters, our own equipment, access to fantastic technical processes, funding for art historical research— but what we did not have was freedom from male dominance. Womanspace was a female-controlled institution. The Feminist Art Program had become a women's program in an institution whose values were shaped by men. Not that the men were anything but supportive, but they controlled the school. Even though they had made space for us, they were not prepared to restructure the school so that it was equalized on all levels.

Then, the Feminist Art Program's first graduate student put a painting into the annual graduate show. This work clearly reflected all of the values of the program that I supported. It was direct; the subject matter was clear; it related to the woman's own experience; but it was clumsily painted. This is an inevitable step in feminist art education because, as students become successively more connected with themselves as women, they usually go through a stage of making very overt art. This art is often awkward because it is an attempt to articulate feelings for which there is, as yet, no developed form language. As the women develop as artists, they build skills that are relevant to their content. Their work improves and they become more sophisticated, but that sophistication is built on a solid, personal foundation and is not a result of imitating prevailing art modes, something common at Cal Arts as well as at other art schools.

The male faculty in the art school objected to our graduate student's painting; they said things to her that were identical to the things that had been said to me when I was in graduate school. I couldn't believe it. I had started a program for women so that no one would ever have to go through what I had gone through. Now our first graduate was being subjected to the same misunderstanding, prejudice, and blindness that I had been faced with. This problem extended to the entire program. Once the women walked out the door of the Feminist Studio, they were confronted with a set of values that promoted nonexposure of feelings, standards of art that derived from the male art community, and pressure to be "professional," whether that professionalism was real or merely a posture. All of the values of the art school that I had attended were present at Cal Arts, despite their support of a feminist program.

In Fresno, the program was *structured* on new ideas about what it is to be a woman. Because there were no men around to *fight against,* women were liberated from that circumscribed area of either submitting to men or rebelling against them. They were able to simply act positively on their own impluses, something that became increasingly difficult when we were at Cal Arts. Because male values and attitudes pervaded the whole institution, women became confused. When they acted on their own behalf, they violated the standards of the institution. If they conformed to the artmaking values of the institution, they denied themselves as women. This was not as much of a problem for women who had found a synthesis between their own aesthetic and the prevailing male standards, but for women who wanted to work out of their rage, for those who wished to find a way to express direct feelings, for the ones who wanted to use their art to change culture, there was a constant contradiction between the values of the program and those of Cal Arts.

I was forced to ask myself why I had brought the program into this institution in the first place. As ridiculous as the answer was, I had to recognize that I still entertained fantasies that male society would reward me for challenging their values. I also saw that I had not actually realized that the real meaning of the Fresno Program was that it existed *outside the sphere of male dominance* and that it was having a space that was not regulated by men and masculine values that made it possible to be ourselves as women. If we could find a way to make an institution that was coeducational and still not male-dominated, we could function in it. It was not so much an issue of separatism, I concluded, as it was the simple fact of being away from male control. Had Cal Arts been willing to equalize its administration, its courses, its teaching staff, and its student body, the Feminist Art Program, as I conceived of it, could have continued to operate within its walls.

But even if Cal Arts had been willing, someday, to equalize its staff, it would never have equalized its perception of reality. No male institution is yet ready to surrender the fantasy that men's history *is* history. If I had learned anything from my investigation of women's work, it was that we have our own history and that that history, *to me,* is as significant as men's history is to men. The art history classes at Cal Arts, as at all schools, focuses on the work of men, although there was a real effort to include women. But women were included in the context of men's ideas, men's values, and men's past. Or there was art history and then "women in art," which by its very nature trivialized women's art because it emphasized the idea that there is *important art history,* and then, as a sideshow to the main attraction, women's art.

Sure the Feminist Art Program could be a part of Cal Arts, but only if we were willing to "fit in." But another thing I had learned from women's work was that the nature of my oppression as a woman, in my life and in my work, grew out of the fact that I had to "fit into" the values and forms of male culture. Whatever information lay outside of the perspective of that culture *didn't count.* Thus all the material in women's work that grew out of women's experience, even if it was clearly expressed, could not be important within the context of a male-dominated institution, because only those things that were relevant to men were seen as important. However, if women's work is studied as a side issue, then it cannot challenge the fundamental dominance of male world-view. So I was right back where I had started. I had moved forward and then slid backward.

But, during the three years since I had first gone to Fresno, I had grown and changed. If I was not ready to take responsibility in 1970, I was more ready in 1973. It was difficult for me to face leaving the institution, but I could see that I had no choice. I began to think about establishing a women's program that would be entirely independent from any school. But I did not think that I could do that by myself. I felt that I had found my way back to an artmaking that could sustain me for a long time. I knew that I could nourish myself with the work of other women, past and present. I thought about withdrawing from the women's movement, going back into my studio and working entirely on my own work. But what I had learned from history was a hard lesson to forget. All those women doing all that good work and none of it able to affect the culture sufficiently to ensure that their work and its meaning would survive and be effective. Could I accept making work that was strong, personal, feminine, but impotent?

In the fall of 1972, Arlene Raven had moved to Los Angeles. She was an art historian and was drawn to the West Coast and the female art community because she felt that we were building a solid alternative for women in art for the first time in history, something she had wanted to do in the East. For about six months, she and I circled each other warily, trying to make friends, drawing back from the intensity of the relationship, for, in each other, we saw real peers. This was the one thing I had not yet managed to secure for myself. There were, by the fall of 1972, a number of women active in the Los Angeles art community. Many of them were instrumental in the work of opening Womanspace in the winter of that year. But with the exception of Sheila De Bretteville, who established the first women's design program in the country (at Cal Arts), none of them had the same goals as I did: the establishment of an alternative structure that would allow women to take control of the entire artmaking process.

I had come to the conclusion that I would have to leave Cal Arts, and although I was anxious about it, I submitted my resignation early in 1973. I still was not sure whether I would simply withdraw into my own work or try to make the next step, which I believed was the establishment of a feminist program and alternate art structure outside of any male-dominated institution. It was clear to me, through my experience at Cal Arts and from my study of history, that the only alternative to working in private and sustaining my personal point of view by turning to other women's work was to develop a way by which women could control not only their own artmaking process but also what happened to that art when it left the studio. In other words, I had seen that women creators, even when they managed to break through female role and make themselves into artists, still had to funnel their work back into a system of exhibition and distribution that men controlled.

I had experienced this problem in my Fullerton show. Even though I had tried to express my point of view as a woman, it was not apprehended. I had thought then that the problem I was having grew mainly out of the fact that the content of my work was unclear. But examining so much women's work had demonstrated that there were some women, like Virginia Woolf, whose feminist point of view was clear, but whose work, until recently, still was not recognized and valued for what it was. And any thoughts that I had about the misperception of Woolf being an aspect of her historic period were dispelled by my experience at Cal Arts. There, as everywhere in male culture, pressure was placed upon women to conform to male standards. If they succeeded, within the Feminist Art Program, to break through those standards to their own experience, their work was put down for being "obvious."

No, there was no choice. Unless we could control what happened to our art after we made it, we would all be subjected to the same distortion, devaluing, and discrimination that the women before us had suffered. But the job of establishing such an alternative required the mingling of various skills, more skills than I as a single individual possessed. I had known that in Fresno, but had no choice but to shape that Fresno program in relation to my abilities, my perceptions, and my needs. I had no other woman to work with. Mimi and I had formed the Feminist Art Program and found that we had differing points of view, so different that we had to separate. The developing female community was shaping Womanspace in terms of the wide variety of needs in that community, and that was necessary. But to build an entire institution that could offer an alternative to women creators was a job that required the work and the shared vision of several women committed to the idea and value of a female point of view.

In Fresno, I had recognized that not only did there have to be an art program, but also a link-up to our heritage. This demanded an art historian who was willing to break with the nature of the art history profession and who was committed to challenging its values in much the same way I was challenging art values. She would have to be able to reject the standards of male art judgment when those standards were inappropriate to women's work while maintaining a belief in the importance of standards of excellence. The skills of a designer were also crucial, but again a designer who wished to change the traditional relationship designers have to the organizations they serve. Instead of being service-oriented, a designer in the context of an alternate feminist art institution would have to be capable of generating projects that could translate the private world of the creator to the public world of the community. But until 1973, I had not been able to connect with women who shared my goals and vision and had the courage to break with traditional concepts of the art professions. I knew that the old roles of the art-related professions would not work. The art historian/critic could not "serve" the artist in the sense that Lucy Lippard, the East Coast art critic and novelist, meant when she called the critic the "housekeeper" of art. Rather, the art historian/critic would have a crucial role in helping women realize themselves in relation to their history and in terms of new standards for women's art. In fact, this art historian/critic would be a *part of* the process of making new art and new standards, rather than someone who came along after the art was made and wrote about it. The designer would have to be interested in the idea of wedding art and design by using mass-production techniques for the artmaking process, so that images could be made available on a wide scale; for if women creators were to be free of male domination, it was clear that we would have to make work for a female audience, and that audience could not afford the kinds of art prices that the male art community insisted upon.

Additionally, in such a structure, I knew that I as an artist would have a wider responsibility than just making art, as I had had for some time. But in such an alternate context, my violation of the "role" of artist would be expected, rather than be the aberration it appeared in the male art community. I would have to participate in all aspects of the growth of such an alternate art structure and use my ability to conceptualize form to create new social forms as well as aesthetic ones. That responsibility no longer frightened me as much as it had in the past, although, I must say, I became somewhat weary of people asking me, "When do you get a chance to paint?" I might have made a new self-definition as an artist, but the same old stereotypes about artists persisted, just as they did about women.

However, I knew that by involving myself in doing things an artist is "not supposed to do," becoming politically active, lecturing, teaching, organizing, I had expanded my self-definition. I had seen myself as a "person" in the world, acting on that world, unafraid to act, and in so doing, not only had I broken through the restrictions of the "artist" role, but more importantly, through those of "female role." Becoming a larger person made me a better artist. But that process of moving into the world, acting in and on it, is something that many women artists are afraid to do, feeling that they will lose something if they leave their studio. I admit it is a risk to spend a lot of time away from the studio, but it is a risk that has been very beneficial to me. Being an artist allows one to be immersed in personal fantasy. That is a positive thing if that fantasy then reaches out into the world and illuminates human fantasy. But because female role has demanded that women stay immersed in the "private," many women have never made the link-up in their work between their personal fantasy and the larger human world. Thus their work remains isolated within the sphere of the female even while they act, by making art, outside of that sphere.

When I decided to leave Cal Arts, I spoke to Arlene about the idea of establishing a feminist program outside of any school. I sort of hoped that she would be uninterested, as that would get me off the hook. Although I was prepared to take greater responsibility, I would have been happy to avoid it and just retreat to my studio. At least, that's what I told myself. However, she thought it was a terrific idea and spoke about her dissatisfaction with the Feminist Art Program at Cal Arts, with which she was also involved by that time. She too felt that it was necessary to create a structure that would allow women to take control of all the art-related professions and mold them into disciplines that could reflect *both* male and female point of view. Her developing knowledge of women's art history had led her to the same conclusion I had reached: that women's work had to be seen in its own context or it would be diminished.

She and I spoke with Sheila, the only feminist designer we felt might be interested in an independent feminist program. I had first met Sheila when the Fresno women and I did the *Everywoman* issue. Mimi, who was working with us then, contributed two articles to the edition. She also introduced me to Sheila, who had agreed to design the paper. I was very impressed by Sheila's idea of making a new form for the new content of women's experience. Sheila established a design format for the newspaper that reflected the equalized structure of the group process I used in Fresno. She gave each woman in the program an equal amount of space in the paper, and, through the design, an equal visual impact. She wanted the form of the publication to itself convey the varying personalities and points of view of the women. She didn't want to use design as it is often used—to manipulate material into a hierarchy of importance.

After working with us, Sheila decided to establish the first feminist design program in the country at Cal Arts. She wanted to explore the implications of feminism for design methodology. She felt that the prevailing myth of the creative individual who worked in isolation often restricted rather than stimulated women's creative process; for many women are isolated, and yet they can't act creatively in their isolation. She felt that this might be a result of women's doubts about themselves. She thought that if she brought a group of women together and helped them work in the same space, either individually or collectively, they might become more comfortable with themselves and hence more confident. This process might then, she reasoned, aid in developing forms that could make the private experience of women become public and communicable to the society. She made considerable strides in creating a feminist design process, but by 1973, she, as well as Arlene and I, had concluded that it was impossible to have a feminist program within a male-dominated school unless one were willing to struggle with men and also compromise considerably.

It was not that the men's attitudes could not be changed, but rather that if one spent time and energy changing those attitudes, one could not direct oneself to the development of new forms and values, something all of us agreed was essential to the formulation and expression of female experience. We realized that the three of us had come to the same point in our thinking. Sheila also believed that there was a female point of view in women's work and in women's perception of the world, and she was committed to the introduction of that point of view into the culture. Arlene wanted to establish new theory for dealing with women's art, and had come across the country because she realized that she needed support to accomplish the goals that she had. All three of us recognized the necessity for merging art disciplines. It was clear to us that in order for any of us to develop "new forms for new content," we had to join forces and address ourselves to making a multifaceted program that could open up new creative options.

We decided to establish the Feminist Studio Workshop. It would be the first entirely independent alternate structure for women in the art-related professions. We had all been working primarily with women in undergraduate school. A number of feminist programs had developed around the country as a result of our West Coast programs. We had other needs, and we all felt that programs in colleges would continue to develop. All of us had found that many young women in college had not yet faced their real situation as women in the culture, having been somewhat protected by being in school. When I started the Fresno Program I had simply assumed that the women in the program would first develop themselves and then naturally commit themselves to help other women develop. This had not been the case. Both in Fresno and at Cal Arts, a number of women were perfectly content to strengthen themselves as artists and then pursue their personal ambitions.

I was very disturbed by this because I did not want to be a casualty of the women's movement. I felt that I as an artist needed other women to help me just as much as they needed me to help them. If I committed myself to the idea of developing a female art, being involved with female education, and changing the values of the culture, I felt that I had a right to expect the same commitment from other women, particularly those who had been aided in their development by the work of women in the movement. It seemed unfair to me for women to benefit from the women's movement and from my work particularly and then refuse to give back their gains to other women. I discussed this with Sheila and Arlene, and we decided to build that demand into our program. We felt that the reason some women who had come through a feminist program did not then contribute to the development of other women probably had something to do with the youth of those women. Because they had not yet struggled in the world, they were unable to comprehend that they had a responsibility to use what they had learned, not only for their personal growth, but to continue the work of changing society's values.

Therefore we decided to direct the Feminist Studio Workshop toward women who already possessed a level of consciousness, some degree of skills, and some commitment to feminism. We wanted to offer them a support environment that would allow them to work out of their experiences as women and develop ways of making that work act upon the culture. Because we three had become involved in female education partly out of our own needs, we wanted the environment to function as much for us as for the students. By developing women who could be leaders, we hoped to share the burden of the responsibility we had taken on, and together push the boundaries of the notion of "new form for new content."

In our previous teaching, all three of us had used a process that we later termed "organic education." This process grew rather naturally out of the principles of the women's movement, as exemplified in consciousness-raising, which allows each woman the time and space necessary for her to assert her real identity and feelings. We were all agreed that all of us would define our interests, our limits, and our goals, and then meet on whatever common ground existed among us, rather than on the basis of subjects that are "supposed to be taught." We structured the program so that it would be open-ended and able to accommodate a variety of needs. One of our firmest principles was that whenever a number of needs arose that could be seen as conflicting, we would not approach them in terms of which needs are the most important, thus denying some while acknowledging others, but rather by asking: How can we accommodate everyone's needs?

We all agreed that it was essential for our students to understand their historical circumstances, to perceive their real
situation as women and as female creators, and to not have
expectations that would be appropriate to men's historical
condition, but not women's. We were committed to helping
female creators develop new forms, make new kinds of work,
and take responsibility to put that work out in the world,
make a context for it, secure its effectiveness, and help other
women do the same for themselves. I use the term "female
creator" advisedly, because we felt that once women had
new expressive options, they might very well make themselves
into new kinds of artists, for whom a new term might be
useful.

In order for a "female creator" to emerge, one who could
develop a "new style," she would have to have a variety of
skills, something women in the arts are not now encouraged to
develop. Since we planned to work out of a content base,
which would allow the fusing of emotion and idea, we intended to ask women to think about all the possible ways they
might express their subject matter and then help them learn
whatever techniques were necessary for the realization of their
ideas. Since women would be required to familiarize themselves with the work of women of the past, they would need
methodological and research skills, as there is still so little information on women's work available. We felt that the women
needed to be able to write about their work and that of other
women so that, if they found themselves in a situation like
Anaïs Nin faced—that is, the absence of any critical response
to her work—then they could get together to write about
each other's work. If they ever wanted to publish their criticism, they would need to know rudimentary graphic and
design skills and be able to photograph their work for repro-
duction in the publication. We wanted to train women to

educate other women, to move out into the world and establish classes based upon the techniques that had helped them to become independent, confident, and productive human beings. We tried to assess the needs of women in the arts and address ourselves to changing the society so that women's work would no longer be mitigated against on any level.

We all recognized that traditional role concepts were destructive to the development of a feminist alternative. Just as we had all felt constricted by female role, we also felt constricted by the professional roles we were forced to play within the male institution. A female institution, as we three were conceiving it, would be based upon the principle of flexible role-relationships, for if we wanted to address ourselves to the needs of women, we felt it was necessary to restructure all concepts of what it is to be a woman and an artist. Flexibility in professional role-relationships was something that seemed impossible to achieve within male-dominated institutions. The professions isolate people and force them to function in terms of professional "roles" rather than as people. In fact, generally, role-playing in male society freezes people into shapes that are not necessarily congruent with their real identities. But it was not the fact of role-playing itself that upset us, but rather that roles were pervaded with positions of dominance and submission. Just as dominance insinuates itself into the relationships between men and women, so it was inherent in all the relationships in the art school and the art professions. The dean is dominant over the faculty; the teacher over the student; the museum director over the curator; the gallery owner over the artist; and whoever is in the (male) dominant position victimizes the person in the (female) powerless position.

Virginia Woolf observed the confining atmosphere of the

professions. She wrote: "If people are highly successful in their professions they lose their senses. Sight goes. They have no time to look at pictures. Sound goes. They have no time to listen to music. Speech goes. They have no time for conversation. They lose their sense of proportion—the relations between one thing and another. Humanity goes. . . . *And so competitive do they become that they will not share their work with others though they have more than they can do themselves* [emphasis mine]. What then remains of a human being who has lost sight, sound, and sense of proportion? Only a cripple in a cave."[1] She then goes on to ask: "How can we enter the professions and yet remain civilized human beings?"[2] The answer, for the three of us, was to redefine the professions.

Although I knew that Sheila and Arlene were women with whom I could build a truly feminist art community, I was scared. I had had many experiences of being disappointed by women, and even brutally rejected. One woman I had helped demonstrated her new-found personal strength by abruptly ending our relationship without any explanation. I was afraid to reach out again. Also, I had learned to nourish myself by nourishing others. I had done this out of necessity because just as my strength, power, and vision had frightened men, it had also frightened some women. Many of the women in the female community were afraid to be too closely identified with me, although they were certainly not afraid to take advantage of the new atmosphere for women artists that I was partially responsible for creating. But, having faced up to male stereotypes and misperceptions of me, I was able to stand up to those same distorted attitudes that emanated from women, although it hurt more when it came from women. *Most peo-*

[1] *Three Guineas* (New York: Harcourt, Brace & Company, 1938), pp. 131–32.
[2] Ibid.

ple, I realized, had been conditioned to think that some personality traits were "male" while others were "female." There seem to be few people in the culture who can apprehend a "person" rather than a "sex."

Because Sheila and Arlene were my peers, I knew that a relationship with them would require me to share in a way that I had never been able to with women. Generally, I had been the "strongest" woman in any group, and so had they. The only time that was not true for me was in my relationship with Mimi, but that was so riddled with a mother/daughter tension that we were never really able to operate as peers, although I wanted to. With Sheila and Arlene, there had to be an end to roles altogether—we had to struggle to see each other as human beings with particular strengths and weaknesses, talents and limitations. Only in an environment that allowed us to escape the stereotypical definitions of women could we see ourselves in our full humanity, something we all desired. Being the "strongest" had allowed me to protect myself from being hurt by the fact that, with the exception of Lloyd, so few people had been willing to accept the fact that I was really the honest, committed woman I knew myself to be.

Often, when I lecture and describe my ideas about feminist education, I am asked why we don't allow men in our programs. The answer is that most men do not seem ready to abandon rigid concepts of "masculinity" and "femininity," and few seem to be able to conceive of a society in which some people are not dominant over others. In fact, some of the fear of the women's movement grows out of the fantasy many men have that we are after role-reversal, that the women's movement really means that women will dominate men, something that doesn't interest most of us at all. Also, men have been conditioned to take control of the situations they are in. Because of that, we cannot have men in a female institution until they are ready to learn new patterns of behavior. At that time, we can slowly bring men into our structure and teach them to function in a new way, a way that does not allow either sex to dominate the other. But we in the workshop cannot do that until the structure we are building is stable and secure.

I struggled with Arlene more than with Sheila, because Sheila resists confrontation. Struggling with Arlene was ultimately the means through which we arrived at a solid, loving relationship. Just as my struggle with Lloyd had allowed us to realize our respective independence and mutual love, so the struggle with Arlene allowed us to confront each other on the most fundamental human level, look at each other, and see ourselves reflected in each other's eyes as full human beings. Sheila is committed to coming to closeness through other means than struggle. My relationship with her grew slowly and methodically, which has allowed us to work out aspects of our interaction more gradually. But Arlene and I went through a struggle that was actually similar to the one I had undergone with Lloyd. We fought and argued, cried and tested, battled each other for primacy, and finally acknowledged each other's identity. The similarity between the struggle with Lloyd and the one with Arlene made me think that perhaps what I had gone through with both of them was a metaphor for the struggle our whole society has to go through in order to break out of the separations of sex and class.

We came together, Sheila, Arlene, and I, in terms of our shared goals, principles, and work. It didn't matter if we became angry with each other, disagreed, shouted, struggled. We were wedded together on the basis of mutual work and goals. And that is what the workshop tries to help its students learn. Women can and must cross over to each other, not just on the basis of our common experience as women, but on the basis of our shared visions as well. Together, we women *can* shape the society to meet our needs, but only if we can put aside the social conditioning that tells us we have to be "nice, personable, and friendly." This doesn't mean we have to be "bastards," but rather that we learn to measure our lives in terms of producing good work and affecting the culture rather than in relationship to the quality of our personalities.

I think that one significant thing that happened to me out of all of this was that my relationship with Arlene and Sheila allowed me to be myself in a public situation. The only other person this has been possible with is Lloyd, and of course that is on a private level. My work with Arlene and Sheila brought me into the world and allowed me to have a place where I was seen as a "person" by women who were my peers. They did not become frightened by my strength, my courage, my determination. Rather, they identified with them and appreciated them because they helped us achieve our common goals.

In the fall of 1973, the Feminist Studio Workshop opened in Los Angeles with thirty women from around the country. Their ages ranged from twenty-two to fifty-two, and they came to the workshop for a variety of reasons, but they all shared a desire to work in a feminist context. Arlene, Sheila, and I had planned that the school would be the first step in establishing an entire alternate art structure. We thought we might move near Womanspace in order to develop a strong sense of community. Shortly before the workshop was to begin, a woman named Edie Gross came to see us with a proposal. She suggested that Womanspace, which needed larger quarters, and the Feminist Studio Workshop rent an old art school near downtown Los Angeles. We thought that was a terrific idea and then, when we discussed it, felt that it would be even better to bring together a number of feminist art organizations that already existed in the city, thereby establishing a rich environment that housed multiple points of view within a feminist context.

Arlene, Sheila, and I had established the workshop as a nonprofit educational corporation, and the corporation was able to rent the building. Then we sublet to a number of groups. It was an important decision to make the workshop part of a community from its inception. The fact of the singularity of the Fresno Program was one of the reasons I had brought it to Cal Arts, in an effort to gain a context. But it was definitely the wrong context. Womanspace had suffered from being a single institution because it, by itself, could not meet all the various needs of the female art community, while maintaining enough credibility as an art organization to affect aesthetic values. Male institutions are reinforced by the very fact that they exist in the context of male culture. But just as one woman's work could not by itself overturn all the cultural values that denied it, a single women's institution could not exert enough influence to act as a new model for social structures and also challenge the values of the old structure.

On November 28, 1973, we opened the Woman's Building, named after the first Woman's Building at the 1893 World's Columbian Exposition at Chicago. Edie Gross, who first thought of uniting the FSW and Womanspace in one structure, became the building's manager and guided it into existence. When the Woman's Building opened, it housed, in addition to the Workshop and Womanspace, a women's cooperative gallery, Grandview, which represents forty women artists; and Gallery 707, a private women's gallery established earlier and then moved to the building. Womanspace expanded and had a group gallery, a one-woman gallery, and an open wall gallery for which women simply signed up. We wanted to provide a variety of choices by which a woman artist could make herself visible. Some women are comfortable bringing their work to a dealer; others prefer to submit their paintings and sculptures to a jury of their peers (Womanspace offered a juried show every year); still others like to simply sign up to show.

In addition, the building housed the Sisterhood Bookstore, a feminist outlet for women's literature, several women's performing groups, and the Associated Women's Press, a network of women's journals. Several political groups rented space in the building—NOW and the Women's Liberation Union, assuring that the exhibition of women's work could take place in an environment that was connected to a wider female community. There are plans to develop a feminist resource library on women's art and a graphics center that will allow the production of a variety of images, in various forms —books, posters, prints, hand-made lithographs. But all those plans are still in the future. By November 1973, we at least had a home for the female culture that was exploding all around us.

When the building opened, my exhibition "The Great Ladies" also opened. For the first time, my work was in a context that could really illuminate it. When I brought my paintings to the gallery (I showed in the women's co-operative), I found a note on the door. It was from one of the women in the workshop. She and several other women wanted to help me install my show. I thought about my previous show at a prestigious male gallery. The Fresno series "Flesh Gardens" was exhibited there. They were heavy paintings. The men who were hanging them made continual comments about the size and weight of the paintings, my size, my sex. I felt so uncomfortable. Even there, in the presence of my accomplishments, I was not able to escape the contempt men felt for women. The contrast was overwhelming. Installing my show at the Woman's Building was a joy. Women dropped in, helped, responded enthusiastically. Arlene had suggested, since my paintings had writing on them, that I also write on the wall, thus tying all the work together.

It took several days to install the show and do the writing. On one wall of the exhibition, I wrote these words:

> The Great Ladies—begun in the Fall of 1972, completed in the Summer of 1973; these women represent themselves, aspects of myself, and various ways in which women have accommodated themselves to the constraints of their circumstances. Some years ago, I began to read women's literature, study women's art, and examine the lives of women who lived before me. I wanted to find role models, to discover how my predecessors had dealt with their oppression as women. I was also searching for clues in their work—clues that could aid me in my art. I wanted to speak out of my femaleness, to make art out of the very thing that made me the "other" in male society. I developed an increasing identification with other women, both those who lived before me and those who, like me, felt the need for a female support community. Together, we built an al-

ternative art institution—the Woman's Building. My paintings can only be fully understood in this new context we have made. I want to thank all those who helped me install my show. This was the first time I've received such remarkable support and I feel honored to be a part of the reappearance of the Woman's Building, 80 years after it was first established in my home town.

For a solid month before the opening, I suffered from depressions, anxiety attacks, even rashes. I felt that the opening of the building and the exhibition of my new work truly revealed my commitment, my ideas, and my values, and I was afraid that they would be rejected. Five thousand people attended the opening. I could hardly believe the crowds when I arrived. I walked up to the gallery that housed my show, and people embraced me and cried and told me how moved they were by what I'd done. I couldn't believe it. I was being myself—really myself—and not only was nothing terrible happening, but I was receiving the acknowledgment I had been deprived of for so long.

The opening of the Woman's Building marked the fulfillment of all the dreams I had when I left the isolation of my studio to go to Fresno. I found my way back to my life as an artist through my identification with other women, and together with them was able to see the realization of a female art community that could house the hopes, the values, and the aspirations of all of us. The Woman's Building is a long way from becoming a permanent alternative institution. But it is a beginning . . . its form may evolve and change, its structure may fade and even die, but its spirit is destined to continue until we have a society that is not dominated by values that lock us all, male and female alike, into stifling and dehumanized roles. Working to build the female art community in Los Angeles helped me to expand my own self-image, to experience myself in ways that are simply not possible within the present structure of male-dominated society, where women's power is seen, if not negatively, then certainly stereotypically. In fact, male society makes women feel as if their power is *not needed or valued,* whereas in the female community, women's power is essential. This drastically changes the way one experiences oneself as woman, as one is valued for the *development* of one's capacities, rather than for the repression of them. And the development of strength does not, in a feminist environment, require the suppression of feeling. This is profoundly liberating, at least it was for me. The female community also made it possible for me to sort out which aspects of my personal pain and hurt were a result of sexism and which grew out of the human condition itself.

Moreover, the female art community provided a context in which I could explore my "feminine qualities," not as aspects of female role, which I always and rightfully rejected, but rather as attributes of my humanity. I was able to see that many of the personality traits that are inculcated into women and then disparaged by male culture (heightened intuition, emotional responsiveness, etc.) are actually valuable *human* abilities, which, if developed by *both* men and women, would greatly improve our society and the relationship between the sexes. My experiences and attitudes as a woman thus became not only positive in and of themselves, but also as a model for the future. "Society and the arts can be rejuvenated only by restoring the despised feminine elements to their proper place among the faculties of man. It follows that women, the chief bearers of the feminine qualities, have a mission to bring about this regeneration, a mission for which their long martyrdom has made them especially fit."[3]

The existence of the Woman's Building, my Grandview show, my experiences over the years in building a female community all combined to make me feel considerably more comfortable about being and expressing myself as a woman in my life and in my art. Finally, in the spring of 1974, I made a real breakthrough in my work. I found a way to convey clearly the content that was still hidden in my earlier images. This made me realize that I had been involved in a process, a process which had allowed me first to experience myself, then express myself fully, a process that has rarely been available to women and which, in my estimation, is simply not possible in a male-dominated situation. Once I could actually be myself and express my point of view, both personally and professionally, I recognized that *through my art,* I could contribute my values and attitudes as a woman to the culture in such a way that I could *affect* the society. Because, as women, we actually have access to the mechanisms of society and because we are more than one half the population, we *can change and mold our environment,* but only if we can be ourselves and express our real points of view. Moving "through the flower" is a process that is available to all of us, a process that can lead us to a place where we can express our humanity and values as women *through our work* and in our lives and in so doing, perhaps we can also reach across the great gulf between masculine and feminine and gently, tenderly, but firmly heal it.

[3] Herbert Marder, *Feminism and Art,* p. 59

Appendix

‿

PERFORMANCE PIECES

Three Women. Feminist Art Program Performance Group. Performed at Womanhouse by Nancy Youdelman, Shawnee Wollenmann, and Jan Oxenberg

This piece grew out of the lives of each of the women in the group. They imagined what would have happened if their lives had taken a different twist. It also grew out of an informal session in role-playing, where we all put on costumes and makeup. Here is a short excerpt from the monologue of each of the three women:

Sparkyl: "You see, my mother was a romantic . . . stars in her eyes and blisters on her fingers. . . . I'm never gonna' be like my mother; no, not me, I'm smart. I wear my stars on my boobs, not in my eyes" [referring to the stars on her costume]. . . . All out front, that's the way *I* want it; you lay your money on the table, baby, I'll lay my body on the bed, simple as that."

Rainbow: "They asked me if I wanted some reds. I said, no, I wasn't into reds at this time . . . they took me into the shower, took off my clothes, and started washing me . . . then they forced this big handful of reds down my throat and car-

ried me into the bedroom . . . they all took turns balling me
. . . when I woke up, all my clothes were gone . . . it was
really a bummer, man . . . but, you gotta stay above it,
man, you gotta have love, or you can really get brung down
. . . yeah, love and acid, man, that's where it's at."
Roslyn: "I mean, I know I've really been fucked over by some
bad men, but I can't believe they're *all* like that. Somewhere,
if I keep looking, I know, I'll find a man who can really appreciate me . . . cause I can do a lot for a man."

Cock and Cunt play, written by Judy Chicago in 1970. Performed at Womanhouse
by Faith Wilding and Jan Lester

The *Cock and Cunt* play is to be performed in a highly
stylized manner. Words are to be spoken haltingly and in
stilted form. Poses and movements should be awkward, slow,
and jerky, resembling puppet motion. Arms and legs are held
akimbo, palms upright and feet pointing out. Voices are
highly exaggerated and in sing-song rhythm with the body
movements. Male voice is low and authoritarian. Female voice
is high and obsequious.

ACT I

Two women, dressed identically in black leotards, enter stage
left. On stage right is large sink full of dirty dishes. Stage
center, an oversize bed. Regular lighting. Stage is merely one
end of a large room with audience seated on floor facing performers.
First woman (SHE) has a plastic vagina strapped to her
crotch. SHE crosses stage to sink, turns and faces audience,
head turned toward second woman (HE), who has followed

SHE across stage and stopped beside her, also facing audience.
HE has a plastic phallus strapped to his crotch.

Lights darken. Single spot on performers and sink.

SHE   "Will you help me do the dishes?"

HE   (Shocked) "Help you do the dishes?"

SHE   "Well, they're your dishes as much as mine!"

HE   "But you don't have a cock!" (grasps cock and begins
     stroking it proudly)

SHE   "What's that got to do with it?"

HE   "A cock means you don't wash dishes. You have a cunt.
     A cunt means you wash dishes."

SHE   (looking at cunt) "I don't see where it says that on my
     cunt."

HE   (pointing at her cunt) "Stu-upid, your cunt/pussy/
     gash/hole or whatever it is, is round like a dish. Therefore
     it's only right for you to wash dishes. My cock is long
     and hard and straight and meant to shoot like guns or
     missiles. Anyone can see that." (*emphasis on cock, long,*
     hard, straight shoot; strokes cock on each emphasis)

(HE turns toward SHE, begins to move in erotic manner, as if
having sexual relations. SHE follows his motion, still in one-
two rhythm).

     "Speaking of shooting, I need to shoot—off, that is, you
     know—drop my load, shoot my wad, get my rocks off—
     you know—I *have* to; I *have* to; you know; *come,* that
     is. I *have* to, no matter what—*I have to come!*"

(voice becomes progressively louder—last phrase said facing
audience) HE and SHE walk in jerky manner in line to bed.
HE mounts SHE (spotlight on bed)

ACT II

SHE lying spread-eagled on bed with head hung over end of
bed toward audience, smiling deliriously. HE is on top of her

with his plastic phallus in her plastic vagina, humping her mechanically, eyes glazed but looking into audience.

HE   (voice building to crescendo) *"I-I-I—me-me-me—I have to—I need to— I must—I-I-I-I—I!"* (falls on her gasping, as if after climax)

Silence. Couple get up mechanically and walk as before to stand in front of bed.

ACT III

Single spot. Couple standing center stage in front of bed.

SHE   "Was it all right? Did I do it right?"

HE   "Yes, yes, it was fine. Now let's go to sleep."

SHE   (almost wistfully) "You know, sometimes I wish I could come too."

HE   (reprimandingly) "Now, you know you don't need to come like I do. Your cunt is made to receive."

SHE   (slowly, in sing-song voice)

"I know.

My cunt is made to receive.

My cunt has an opening in the middle.

Therefore, I must receive.

My cunt is shaped like a dish.

Therefore I must wash dishes."

(beginning to sing)

"My cunt has an opening in the middle.

Therefore I must receive.

My cunt is shaped like a dish.

Therefore I must wash dishes."

(next verse sung five times, singing becoming louder and shriller, like a cantata)

"I have a cunt.

I must receive.

> I have a cunt.
> I must wash dishes."

HE begins to speak simultaneously with first verse of cantata. (in sing-song voice, low tones)

> "I have a cock.
> It is long and hard and straight.
> It is shaped like a gun or missile.
> Therefore I must shoot.
> I must shoot, I must shoot.
> I have a cock."

(next verse sung three or four times) HE stops. SHE continues singing, HE glares at her for several bars. SHE, embarrassed, stops.

> "I have a cock.
> I must shoot.
> I must shoot.
> I have a cock."

HE   "You know, if you keep all this up, making all these demands on me, like asking me to help with the dishes, and wanting to come and everything—you're going to castrate me."

SHE   (timidly) "Castrate you?"

HE   "*Yes,* castrate me!"

SHE   (scared) "Castrate you?"

HE   "*Yes, castrate, castrate . . . castration!*

As he says this last phrase, screaming, he rips off his plastic phallus and begins chasing after her, hitting her with his cock. Lights are all on. As they run, he keeps yelling "castrate," "castration," "castrate me." As they run they knock dishes off sink, pull bedding off bed until SHE sinks to her knees in a pile of bedding. HE keeps beating her fiercely until SHE slumps and dies, lying straight out with the bedding twisted around her. HE glares at her body self-righteously with pursed lips, and in an inhalating stance, puts one foot on her body and triumphantly puts his arm in a salute, flexing his whole torso in victory.

HE and SHE rise, walk off stage right, in puppet fashion.

End

Note—This piece is also very effective as a consciousness-raising technique. In order to employ it as such, one can use a number of methods. (1) Separate the group into "male" and "female." Pass out a Xerox copy of the play to everyone. After they have read it, ask each group to read their parts together, alternating, as the script does, between the male part and the female part. Do this several times until everyone becomes familiar with the words. Then begin clapping hands in a brisk one-two, one-two rhythm. Everyone then reads the words along with that rhythm until the play goes very smoothly, with everyone performing it together. (2) Make a line of all the people in the group. Pass out the script. Then begin to walk around the room, lifting legs in the one-two, one-two rhythm. Perform the entire play together, walking around the room in a circle until everyone feels comfortable. Then ask people to split up into teams of two. All the teams can then work on the play, each person taking the male role and then the female role. After about thirty minutes of practice, ask the teams to perform the play, one team at a time. Each team should perform the play twice so that everyone gets a chance to play both roles. (3) Pass out the script to everyone assembled. Ask them to make up their own teams. Show them how to perform the piece in puppetlike fashion. Then let each team practice in a separate part of the building. Move from team to team and help each couple. After a while, ask the group to reassemble, and ask for volunteer teams to perform the piece. If none volunteers, pick several teams to put the piece on.

Whichever method is used, after the performance, it is very important to have a discussion, preferably using consciousness-raising techniques. The questions to be discussed might be: Which part did you like better? Why? How did you feel about playing a "man"/about playing a "woman"? Usually, the problems that developed in the process of performing the piece indicate the difficulties women have in being assertive, their own sexuality, being used by men, sharing housework. Whatever problems are mentioned by the women after they have performed the play would be useful to discuss, either at that session or a later one.

WAITING

by Faith Wilding

(A female voice speaks in passive, plaintive tone, childlike at first, becoming almost desperate at adolescence, tender at motherhood, and then very slow and cracked in age.)

Waiting . . . waiting . . . waiting . . .
Waiting for someone to come in
Waiting for someone to pick me up
Waiting for someone to hold me
Waiting for someone to feed me
Waiting for someone to change my diaper. Waiting . . .
Waiting to crawl, to walk, waiting to talk
Waiting to be cuddled
Waiting for someone to take me outside
Waiting for someone to play with me
Waiting for someone to put me on the toilet

Waiting for someone to read to me, dress me, tie my shoes
Waiting for Mommy to brush my hair
Waiting for her to curl my hair
Waiting to wear my frilly dress
Waiting to be a pretty girl
Waiting to sit on Daddy's lap. Waiting . . .
Waiting for my new school clothes
Waiting for someone to take me to school
Waiting to stay up until seven o'clock
Waiting to be a big girl
Waiting to grow up. Waiting . . .

Waiting for my breasts to develop
Waiting to wear a bra
Waiting to menstruate
Waiting to read forbidden books
Waiting to stop being clumsy
Waiting to have a good figure
Waiting for my first date
Waiting to have a boyfriend
Waiting to go to a party, to be asked to dance, to dance close
Waiting to be beautiful
Waiting for the secret
Waiting for life to begin. Waiting . . .
Waiting to be somebody
Waiting to wear makeup
Waiting for my pimples to go away
Waiting to wear lipstick, to wear high heels and stockings
Waiting to get dressed up, to shave my legs
Waiting to be pretty. Waiting . . .
Waiting for him to notice me, to call me
Waiting for him to ask me out

Waiting for him to pay attention to me
Waiting for him to fall in love with me
Waiting for him to kiss me, touch me, touch my breasts
Waiting for him to pass my house
Waiting for him to tell me I'm beautiful
Waiting for him to ask me to go steady
Waiting to neck, to make out, waiting to go all the way
Waiting to smoke, to drink, to stay out late
Waiting to be a woman. Waiting . . .
Waiting for my great love
Waiting for the perfect man
Waiting for Mr. Right. Waiting . . .

Waiting to get married
Waiting for my wedding day
Waiting for my wedding night
Waiting for sex
Waiting for him to make the first move
Waiting for him to excite me
Waiting for him to give me pleasure
Waiting for him to give me an orgasm. Waiting . . .
Waiting for him to come home, to fill my time. Waiting . . .
Waiting for my baby to come
Waiting for my belly to swell
Waiting for my breasts to fill with milk
Waiting to feel my baby move
Waiting for my legs to stop swelling
Waiting for the first contractions
Waiting for the contractions to end
Waiting for the head to emerge
Waiting for the first scream, the afterbirth
Waiting to hold my baby

Waiting for my baby to suck my milk
Waiting for my baby to stop crying
Waiting for my baby to sleep through the night
Waiting for my breasts to dry up
Waiting to get my figure back, for the stretch marks to go
    away
Waiting for some time to myself
Waiting to be beautiful again
Waiting for my child to go to school
Waiting for life to begin. Waiting . . .

Waiting for my children to come home from school
Waiting for them to grow up, to leave home
Waiting to be myself
Waiting for excitement
Waiting for him to tell me something interesting, to ask me
    how I feel
Waiting for him to stop being crabby, reach for my hand, kiss
    me good morning
Waiting for fulfillment
Waiting for the children to marry
Waiting for something to happen. Waiting . . .
Waiting to lose weight
Waiting for the first gray hair
Waiting for menopause
Waiting to grow wise
Waiting . . .

Waiting for my body to break down, to get ugly
Waiting for my flesh to sag
Waiting for my breasts to shrivel up

anti.

Waiting for a visit from my children, for letters
Waiting for my friends to die.
Waiting for my husband to die. Waiting . . .
Waiting to get sick
Waiting for things to get better
Waiting for winter to end
Waiting for the mirror to tell me I'm old
Waiting for a good bowel movement
Waiting for the pain to go away
Waiting for the struggle to end
Waiting for release
Waiting for morning
Waiting for the end of day
Waiting for sleep. Waiting . . .

Ablutions. Judy Chicago, Suzanne Lacy, Sandra Orgel, Aviva Ramani. Performed in Venice, California, in 1972

Late in the spring, some months after Womanhouse was dismantled, we presented another performance, this time a piece that was performed only once. We used a studio space for the theater and again sat the audience on the floor. The piece was about an hour and a half long. It had grown out of several months' work in the performance workshop, after we had moved into our studio at school. In the informal performance sessions, several themes had arisen: binding, like Chinese foot-binding, brutalization, rape, immersion, body anxiety, and entrapment. We decided to do a piece that would combine all these issues. *Ablutions* began when the audience entered the room. A tape played throughout the performance of women telling about their experiences of being raped.

Three bathtubs were sitting on the floor, each one filled
with a different, not quite identifiable substance. Around the
tubs, covering an area about fifty feet by twenty feet, were
hundreds of broken egg shells, piles of rope, of kidneys, and
of chain. After about twenty minutes one woman dressed in
jeans and T-shirt led a nude woman to a chair in the back
of the performance space, seated her, and began to slowly
bind her feet, first one, then the other, with a bandagelike
material, and continued binding her over a period of forty
minutes, until she was completely bound, her body tied to
the chair, mummylike.

A few minutes after the binding had begun, another
woman came out and slowly eased herself into the first bathtub, which contained one thousand eggs, with unbroken yolks.
She started to wash herself, allowing the eggs to run down
her body, an image of immersion in her own biology. After
five minutes, she rose and moved on to the second tub, this
one filled with blood, a metaphor for brutalization and at
the same time a reference to menstruation. Another woman
came out and got into the egg tub, and when the first woman
moved on to the third tub, filled with clay, followed her into
the second tub. After the first woman had been in the last
tub for about five minutes, she was lifted out by two other
women. The image, as she rose up from the clay bath, was of
some ancient female fetish figure. The remains of the blood
and the eggs showing through the scaly clay covering made
her seem to be an eerie, mythological figure. She was dried
and wrapped in a sheet, then tied up like a corpse and left,
while the two women did the same thing to the other bather.
While this was going on, a fifth woman appeared and began
to nail kidneys to the wall, at intervals of three feet, all in a
line. The two women, after wrapping the bathers, sat down

face to face, like mirror images, and began to adorn themselves, hanging ropes and chains around their heads in a
strange parody of women at their toiletries.

When the woman doing the binding finished, she began
to tie ropes around the silent, mummified figure in the chair.
Then she started circling the room, tying the ropes to the
tubs, to the prone figures, to the seated women, who were
still covering their heads with ropes and chains. The other
woman finished nailing kidneys to the wall, and then she began tying the kidneys together, pulling the rope tight so that
the blood ran out of the meat and down the wall. Then she
carried the ropes to the bathtubs, the figures, and back again
to the wall. Both women moved slowly, the only action the
roping and tying, the only sound the voices of women relating
the facts of their rapes. Round and round the women walked,
tying everything up neatly, like some obsessive housekeeping
duty, until the performance area was like a spider web and all
the figures caught, contained, bound by their circumstances
and their own self-victimization. The voices on the tape
droned on, repeating the never-ending stories of continual
brutalization, from which there seemed to be no escape. Finally, one woman, then the other, left; the tape continued
for a few more minutes, then ended on a chilling note, the
voice of a woman repeating the words: "I felt so helpless, so
powerless, there was nothing I could do but lay there and cry
softly."

Index

Ney, Elisabet, 149, 166
Nightingale, Florence, 171
Nin, Anaïs, v, ix-xi, xiv, 124, 133–
  34, 160, 162, 176–77, 179, 195
Nochlin, Linda, 149n
Novelists, women, 160–77
NOW, 202
Nuns, as artists, 147
Nurturing. *See* "Mothering" (nur-
  turing)

O'Keeffe, Georgia, 141, 142, 152,
  158, 177
Oppenheim, Merrit, 152
"Organic education," 194–96
Orphism, 152
"Otherness," female, 130, 132,
  143, 144, 146
"OX" (Schapiro), 143
Oxenberg, Jan, 207

Pankhurst, Emmeline, 169
Parent-child relationship, 108–9,
  119–20, 138–40
"Pasadena Lifesavers" (painting),
  56–57, 61, 62, 137, 143, 181
Passivity, female, 122, 125–26
Patriarchal culture. *See* Cultural
  attitudes; Male-dominated value
  structure; Sex-role conditioning
  and stereotypes
Peale, Anna, 149
Peale, Sarah, 149
Performance Workshop, 117–32
Personality structure, women in
  art and, 57, 64–68, 72–92, 93–
  111, 118–32; alternative art
  community and, 186–206
Phallus imagery, women in art
  and use of, 33–35, 36–37, 52–53,
  55
Picasso, Pablo, 31, 152
Plastics, use of, 41–42, 52, 56
Plexiglas, use of, 56
Political activism, women and,
  164–77
"Portrait of Charlotte du Val
  d'Ognes," 149
Pottery, women and, 146, 147

Process art, 62
Professions, art-related, female,
  alternative art community and,
  186–206
Pyrotechnicians, women in art as,
  58–59

Rape, 217–19
Rap Weekend (Fresno, California,
  1971), 144
Raven, Arlene, v, 145, 186, 190–
  92, 197–98, 199–201
Read, Herbert, 144n
"Red Flag" (lithograph), 135–37
Reeves, Nancy, 130n, 147n
Rejection mechanism, women's
  movement and, 110–11
Representational art, women
  artists and, 132, 156–57
Richier, Germaine, 152
Rivalry Play, 89
Robusti, Marietta, 147
Role conditioning. *See* Sex-role
  conditioning and stereotypes
Room of One's Own, A (Woolf),
  166
Runaway to Heaven—A Biography
  of Harriet Beecher Stowe (John-
  ston), 169n
Ruysch, Rachel, 148

Sage, Kay, 152
St. Phalle, Nikki de, 152, 157, 158
Sand, George, 160, 161, 164, 169
Sanger, Margaret, 127, 171
Schapiro, Miriam, 64, 81–86, 89,
  96, 97, 98, 102, 103–11, 112–13,
  139–41, 143–44, 145, 152,
  158n, 188, 191, 198
Sculpture, women and, 149–50,
  152–53
Second Sex, The (Beauvoir), 146n
Self-decoration, female, 121
Self-image (self-identity), women
  and, 54–56, 68, 72–92, 93–111,
  112–32, 135–37, 143–44, 153–59,
  190; history of women's movement and, 164–77; women writers and, 169–77

FOR THE BEST IN PAPERBACKS, LOOK FOR THE

In every corner of the world, on every subject under the sun, Penguin represents quality and variety—the very best in publishing today.

For complete information about books available from Penguin—including Pelicans, Puffins, Peregrines, and Penguin Classics—and how to order them, write to us at the appropriate address below. Please note that for copyright reasons the selection of books varies from country to country.

In the United Kingdom: For a complete list of books available from Penguin in the U.K., please write to *Dept E.P., Penguin Books Ltd, Harmondsworth, Middlesex, UB7 0DA.*

In the United States: For a complete list of books available from Penguin in the U.S., please write to *Consumer Sales, Penguin USA, P.O. Box 999—Dept. 17109, Bergenfield, New Jersey 07621-0120.* VISA and MasterCard holders call 1-800-253-6476 to order all Penguin titles.

In Canada: For a complete list of books available from Penguin in Canada, please write to *Penguin Books Canada Ltd, 10 Alcorn Avenue, Suite 300, Toronto, Ontario, Canada M4V 3B2.*

In Australia: For a complete list of books available from Penguin in Australia, please write to the *Marketing Department, Penguin Books Ltd, P.O. Box 257, Ringwood, Victoria 3134.*

In New Zealand: For a complete list of books available from Penguin in New Zealand, please write to the *Marketing Department, Penguin Books (NZ) Ltd, Private Bag, Takapuna, Auckland 9.*

In India: For a complete list of books available from Penguin, please write to *Penguin Overseas Ltd, 706 Eros Apartments, 56 Nehru Place, New Delhi, 110019.*

In Holland: For a complete list of books available from Penguin in Holland, please write to *Penguin Books Nederland B.V., Postbus 195, NL-1380AD Weesp, Netherlands.*

In Germany: For a complete list of books available from Penguin, please write to *Penguin Books Ltd, Friedrichstrasse 10-12, D-6000 Frankfurt Main I, Federal Republic of Germany.*

In Spain: For a complete list of books available from Penguin in Spain, please write to *Longman, Penguin España, Calle San Nicolas 15, E-28013 Madrid, Spain.*

In Japan: For a complete list of books available from Penguin in Japan, please write to *Longman Penguin Japan Co Ltd, Yamaguchi Building, 2-12-9 Kanda Jimbocho, Chiyoda-Ku, Tokyo 101, Japan.*